Accounting in the Hotel and Catering Industry

Volume 1

Accounting in the Hotel and Catering Industry

Volume 1

Peter J. Harris, MSc, MHCIMA, CDipAF
Principal Lecturer, Department of Hotel, Catering and Food Studies
Oxford Polytechnic

Peter A. Hazzard, MSc, FCMA, AMBIM
Principal Lecturer, Department of Accountancy and Business,
Slough College of Higher Education

Hutchinson
London Melbourne Sydney Auckland Johannesburg

Hutchinson Education

An imprint of Century Hutchinson Ltd
62–65 Chandos Place, London WC2N 4NW

Century Hutchinson Australia Pty Ltd
PO Box 496, 16–22 Church Street, Hawthorn,
Victoria 3122, Australia

Century Hutchinson New Zealand Ltd
PO Box 40–086, Glenfield, Auckland 10, New Zealand

Century Hutchinson South Africa (Pty) Ltd
PO Box 337, Bergvlei, 2012 South Africa

First published by Northwood Publications Ltd 1972
Second edition 1977
Third edition 1979

First published as *Accounting and Financial Management in the
Hotel and Catering Industry*: Volume 1, by Hutchinson, 1983
Fourth edition published 1987

Typeset in 11 on 12 pt Palatino by
Hope Services, Abingdon, Oxon
Printed and bound in Great Britain by
Anchor Brendon Ltd, Tiptree, Essex

British Library Cataloguing in Publication Data
Harris, Peter J.
   Accounting in the hotel and catering
industry.—4th ed.—(Hotel and catering).
1. Hotels, taverns, etc.—Great Britain—
Accounting 2. Caterers and catering—
Great Britain—Accounting
I. Title II. Hazzard, Peter A. III. Harris,
Peter J. Accounting and financial management
in the hotel and catering industry
IV. Series
657'.837'00941   HF5686.H75

ISBN 0–09–172966–1

Contents

Preface to the Fourth Edition

Originally published as *Accounting and Financial Management in the Hotel and Catering Industry*: volume 1, this book has been substantially revised, expanded and updated in an endeavour to keep abreast of modern developments and their applications in the hotel, catering and institutional industry.

In line with previous editions the needs of students studying for hotel, catering and institutional qualifications, executives and management within the industry and the smaller hotelier have been carefully borne in mind throughout this work.

Accounting in the Hotel and Catering Industry provides for the book-keeping and accounting requirements of:
- (a) the hotel reception certificates and diplomas; and
- (b) the ordinary diplomas in hotel, catering and institutional operations, year one.

Its sister volume, *Managerial Accounting in the Hotel and Catering Industry*, provides for the accounting requirements of:
- (a) the HCIMA professional qualification Part B (major study) Financial Management I; and
- (b) the ordinary diplomas in hotel, catering and institutional operations, year two.

The combined volumes provide for the accounting requirements of:
- (a) the higher diplomas in hotel, catering and institutional management;
- (b) the HCIMA professional qualification Part B (major and elective studies) Financial Management I & II; and
- (c) the various degrees in hotel, catering and institutional administration.

Notable changes to this edition are:
1. Chapter 5, Value Added Tax, has been updated.
2. Two new chapters have been added, namely Chapter 15, Cost–Volume–Profit Relationships, and Chapter 16, Introduction to Budgetary Control.

Finally we should like to thank those who have drawn to our attention errors in the earlier editions and made suggestions for inclusion in this edition. As always users' comments are welcome.

P.J.H.

January, 1987
P.A.H.

Certain questions at the end of chapters are reprinted by kind permission of:

Hotel, Catering and Institutional Management Association
(HCIMA)

Chartered Institute of Management Accountants   (CIMA)
Chartered Association of Certified Accountants   (CACA)
Scottish Technical Education Council   (Scotec.)
British Association of Hotel Accountants   (BAHA)

Introduction

The hotel and catering industry has developed into a dynamic, progressive industry following the increase in world-wide demand for its services in recent years. However, expansion attracts competitors into the field and this industry is no exception. Competition eventually eliminates the firm whose operations are not well planned and controlled, whose management takes wrong vital decisions and misses profitable opportunities. The results of such mismanagement are recorded for all to see in the accounting records in the form of poor profit or even a loss, and probably no cash balance with which to pay overdue creditors.

To avoid this sad position and to enable positive action to be taken in developing a business and increasing its value, the right information needs to be available.

It is at this point that the question is asked, 'Have we the necessary information required on which to take action, and are our recording and control techniques adequate to answer the needs of a successful business?' The answer is frequently 'no', particularly in the medium and small enterprises where the trader visualizes complex recording systems and an administrative wage bill of huge proportions. This vision is unwarranted, for the accounting procedures of a business are built around the business, and not the business built around the accounting system. The small business acquires a simple system, the large business one of the larger dimensions.

Accounting information generally serves three purposes, routine external and routine internal reporting as well as non-routine decision making. The following diagram shows this more clearly:

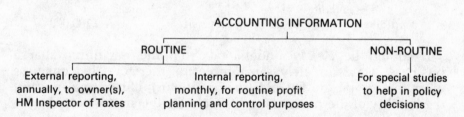

Routine information recorded in the financial accounting system for external reporting is essential for any business, and this is covered comprehensively in Vol. 1.

With an understanding of financial recording the manager needs to consider how his knowledge of accounting can guide him in effective management. Vol. 2 is designed to help him interpret accounting information and to gain a well-rounded understanding of modern management accounting techniques.

In the past hoteliers and caterers have considered and believed an enterprise to be successful provided what was considered a 'satisfactory profit' was attained.

How do we measure the success of a business? Profit at a particular level over a number of years is generally regarded as a measure of success provided it is related to the money invested in a business. A business in which £100,000 is invested achieving a constant profit of £20,000 per year is considerably more successful than one which makes a similar profit after investing £200,000. Financial information is designed to indicate how management action may be taken to increase the return on investment. A large company with a number of hotels will be judged by the performance in terms of profit in relation to its budgeted profit, and its budgeted profit will be set in relation to the investment in the company. Although financial results tend to measure success of the smaller business, the larger the business the more significant do financial considerations enter into the work of management. Management efficiency is ultimately measured by profit achieved on money invested. The efficient business grows and prospers; the inefficient ultimately fails.

By comparing the financial position of a company over a specified period of time, one is able to measure the overall efficiency of the business management. The balance sheet is a device for showing the financial position at any given time, therefore we should consider how the balance sheet is formulated.

G. Gold has an assett of £100,000 in cash. If he invests this sum in a business then the business becomes liable to Mr Gold for the amount invested. Hence the initial financial position shown by the balance sheet may be stated in the following manner:

1. Balance Sheet

Liability		Asset	
Capital	£100,000	Cash	£100,000

It should be clearly understood from the beginning that a business is a completely separate entity, therefore this business owes the capital to Mr Gold (the proprietor), illustrating in effect the liability of the business to Mr Gold for the sum invested.

The next stage is to consider the effect upon the balance sheet of transactions such as: purchasing of premises; purchasing of food; receipt of cash from customers.

2.

Balance Sheet

Buys hotel premises for cash, £60,000

Liabilities		Assets	
	£		£
Capital	100,000	Hotel premises	60,000
		Cash	40,000
	100,000		100,000

3.

Balance Sheet

Purchases the following for cash:
   Kitchen plant £10,000
   Furniture   £20,000

Liabilities		Assets	
	£		£
Capital	100,000	Hotel premises	60,000
		Kitchen plant	10,000
		Furniture	20,000
		Cash	10,000
	100,000		100,000

4.

Balance Sheet

Purchases food for cash, £3,000

Liabilities		Assets	
	£		£
Capital	100,000	Hotel premises	60,000
		Kitchen plant	10,000
		Furniture	20,000
		Food	3,000
		Cash	7,000
	100,000		100,000

5.

Balance Sheet

Sells meals to guests, hence Sales revenue − Cost of sales (food cost) = Profit: £7,500 − £3,000 = £4,500; increasing the worth of the business to £104,500

Liabilities		Assets	
	£		£
Capital	100,000	Hotel premises	60,000
Profit	4,500	Kitchen plant	10,000
		Furniture	20,000
		Cash	14,500
	104,500		104,500

6. Balance Sheet

Purchases more food:
£3,000 on credit
£1,000 for cash   £4,000

Liabilities	£	Assets	£
Capital	100,000	Hotel premises	60,000
Profit	4,500	Kitchen plant	10,000
Creditors	3,000	Furniture	20,000
		Food	4,000
		Cash	13,500
	107,500		107,500

7. Balance Sheet

Meals sold:
£2,000 on credit   £
£8,000 for cash   10,000
Less Cost of sales   4,000
_____
6,000

Liabilities	£	Assets	£
Capital	100,000	Hotel premises	60,000
Profit	10,500	Kitchen plant	10,000
Creditors	3,000	Furniture	20,000
		Debtors	2,000
		Cash	21,500
	113,500		113,500

8. Balance Sheet

Received cash from
debtors, £2,000. Paid
creditors in cash, £3,000.
This reduces the cash
balance by £1,000

Liabilities	£	Assets	£
Capital	100,000	Hotel premises	60,000
Profit	10,500	Kitchen plant	10,000
		Furniture	20,000
		Cash	20,500
	110,500		110,500

9. Balance Sheet

Purchased for cash:
cutlery, glass and china,
£2,500. Modernizing
premises and facilities,
£13,000

Liabilities	£	Assets	£
Capital	100,000	Hotel premises	73,000
Profit	10,500	Kitchen plant	10,000
		Furniture	20,000
		China, glass and cutlery	2,500
		Cash	5,000
	110,500		110,500

Accounting equation

At this point it is useful to introduce the 'accounting equation'. This is represented by a simple formula which highlights the relationship which exists between a firm's capital,* assets and liabilities and may be expressed as:

Capital = Assets − Liabilities

The point about the equation is it shows that a firm's capital is equivalent to the difference between its assets and liabilities. This will be so regardless of the volume of business transactions being undertaken. To illustrate this fact the financial figures of balance sheet numbers 4, 5 and 6 of the preceding text examples have been applied to the accounting equation and tabulated below:

	Capital =	Assets −	Liabilities
	£	£	£
B/S No.			
4	100,000 =	100,000 −	Nil
5	104,500 =	104,500 −	Nil
6	104,500 =	107,500 −	3,000

Having purchased and sold food for cash, i.e. balance sheet numbers 4 and 5, realizing a £4,500 profit, G. Gold's capital increases and is represented by an equivalent increase in cash of £4,500. However, the further purchase of food, i.e. balance sheet number 6, has no effect on Gold's capital, now £104,500, as the increase in assets of £3,000 of stock was offset by the creditors to whom the business is liable for £3,000.

Principles of double entry

The balance sheets above show that on an investment of £100,000 a profit of £10,500 has been made, representing 10½%, which may be considered a reasonable return for the first year. Such balance sheet interpretation is fully dealt with in Vol. 2. The prime concern at this stage is the recording of transactions in a manner so as to eliminate the laborious and wasteful effort in preparing a balance sheet each time a transaction takes place.

However, before this is possible it should be appreciated that every transaction has a twofold aspect:

---

* This includes an owner's capital in business together with any profits realized therein.

'Any' Account

Debit (Dr)	Credit (Cr)
VALUE RECEIVED	VALUE GIVEN

The *debit entry* represents *value received* by the account and the *credit entry* represents *value given* by the account.

To record the twofold aspect of each and every business transaction the principle of double entry is applied. This states that for every debit entry there is an equal and corresponding credit entry.

Taking the example in the balance sheet of G. Gold, who invested £100,000 in a business, the transaction would be recorded as follows:

Dr	Capital a/c	Cr
	Cash	£100,000

Note: the word 'account' is abbreviated a/c

Dr	Cash a/c	Cr
Capital	£100,000	

Thus G. Gold (as shown above) has given value in the sum of £100,000, represented by a credit entry in his account (capital account) in the books of the business, and the business has received the value of £100,000 from G. Gold, represented by a debit entry in the cash account of the business. It is useful at this point to note that *assets* are recorded as *debit entries* and *liabilities* are recorded as *credit entries*. Continuing with the principle of double entry the next transaction of G. Gold would be recorded as follows:

Dr	Hotel Premises a/c	Cr
Cash	£60,000	

Buys hotel premises for cash, £60,000

Dr	Cash a/c	Cr
	Hotel premises	£60,000

Again double entry is completed and the relevant accounts have been debited and credited respectively. The following four transactions of G. Gold would appear as shown below:

Dr	Kitchen Plant a/c	Cr
Cash	£10,000	

Purchases kitchen plant for cash, £10,000

Dr		Cash a/c		Cr
		Kitchen plant		
			£10,000	

Dr		Furniture a/c		Cr
Cash	£20,000			

Purchases furniture for cash, £20,000

Dr		Cash a/c		Cr
		Furniture	£20,000	

Dr		Purchases a/c		Cr
Cash	£3,000			

Purchases food for cash, £3,000

Dr		Cash a/c		Cr
		Purchases	£3,000	

Dr		Sales a/c		Cr
		Cash	£7,500	

Sells meals to guests for cash, £7,500

Dr		Cash a/c		Cr
Sales	£7,500			

From the above illustrations it may be observed that the transactions of G. Gold shown in balance sheets 1 to 5 have been recorded in a clear manner according to the theory of double entry. It is beneficial at this stage to learn another simple rule of book-keeping. This states that transaction entries of a similar nature should be grouped together in one account. Therefore if the foregone accounts are again read it will become apparent that there are six cash entries which in fact would be grouped together in one account in the following manner:

Dr		Cash a/c		Cr
	£			£
Capital	100,000	Hotel		
Sales	7,500	premises	60,000	
		Kitchen		
		plant	10,000	
		Furniture	20,000	
		Purchases	3,000	

Thus the cash account is debited with money received by the business, and credited when money is paid out by the business. Observe that the narrative beside each entry, i.e. capital, sales, kitchen plant, etc., denotes either where the value has come from, e.g. furniture (furniture a/c), or where the value is going to, e.g. sales (sales a/c), whichever the case may be. On completion of recording the transactions, but prior to the preparation of the balance sheet, all accounts are balanced.

Balancing an account

The procedure of balancing applies to all accounts and is dealt with in the following manner:

(a) Total the debit and credit sides of the account (individually).
(b) The difference is calculated and entered on the side with the lower total. This figure is named the 'balance'.
(c) The debit and credit sides of the account are again totalled and found to agree.

This completed, the balance is carried down to the opposite side of the account, thus completing double entry. Below is G. Gold's cash account balanced in the above fashion:

Dr		Cash a/c		Cr	
	£			£	*Note:*
Capital	100,000	Hotel			Abbreviations –
Sales	7,500	premises	60,000		carried down c/d
		Kitchen			brought down b/d
		plant	10,000		
		Furniture	20,000		
		Purchases	3,000		
		Balance c/d	14,500		
	107,500		107,500		
Balance b/d	14,500				

(The difference between the debit and credit (£14,500) = the 'balance' of the account. This balance, although entered on the credit side, is known as a 'debit balance' as it represents the amount by which the total of the entries debited to the account exceeds the total of those credited.)

If each business transaction has been recorded correctly, i.e. debited and credited to the relevant accounts, the sum total of all the debit entries should equal the sum total of all the credit entries. To prove these totals coincide a 'trial balance' is extracted from the ledger.

The construction of a trial balance may be effected by determining the balance of each and every account in the ledger. All the debit balances are then listed in one column, in the trial balance, and all the credit entries listed in a second column. The two columns are totalled and, providing double entry has been completed correctly within the ledger, should agree.

Hence, if it is decided to extract a trial balance from the above set of accounts concerning G. Gold up to the date of balance sheet No. 5, then the result would appear as follows:

Trial Balance

	£	£
Capital		100,000
Hotel premises	60,000	
Kitchen plant	10,000	
Furniture	20,000	
Purchases	3,000	
Sales		7,500
Cash in hand	14,500	
	107,500	107,500

Note: (a) A trial balance *does not* constitute part of the double entry system of book-keeping. It is simply a list of debit and credit balances extracted from the ledger.

(b) When extracting a trial balance it is important to remember the balance is not written in each ledger account but merely calculated and written in the trial balance.

The trial balance is dealt with in greater detail in Chapter 5.

If there is only one entry in an account, e.g. hotel premises a/c, purchases a/c, etc., the balance will equal the amount entered and there is no necessity to balance although it is not incorrect to do so.

If G. Gold's balance sheet is prepared at this stage from his books of account then the following would result:

G. Gold Balance Sheet

Liabilities		Assets	
	£		£
Capital	100,000	Hotel premises	60,000
Profit	4,500	Kitchen plant	10,000
		Furniture	20,000
		Cash	14,500
	104,500		104,500

By comparing this balance sheet with G. Gold's balance sheet No. 5

it will become apparent that the two are identical, confirming the authenticity and convenience of keeping accounts. With regard to the computation of the item 'profit' in the balance sheet this is calculated by the simple formula below:

Profit = Meals at selling price − Food at cost price
£4,500 =   £7,500   −   £3,000

The accounting procedure for preparing and calculating profit will be covered in the chapters dealing with final accounts.

Divisions of the ledger

Traditionally all the accounts of a business should be maintained together in a single binding known as the ledger. This is frequently found to be impractical due to the size and geographical location of the various departments of a business and where there is more than one individual recording transactions. To remedy the problem the ledger is usually divided and sub-divided into workable components, the most widely practised being:

1. *General* (often referred to as *impersonal* or *nominal*) *ledger*, containing all the real and nominal accounts.

2. *Bought* (sometimes referred to as the *purchases* or *creditors*) *ledger*, accommodating all the personal accounts of suppliers (creditors).

3. *Sales* (or *debtors*) *ledger*, comprising all the personal accounts of customers (debtors).

The purchases and sales ledgers are frequently sub-divided into geographical location, or alphabetically, according to the needs of a particular business. The proprietor of a business may require certain accounts of a confidential nature to be kept in what is described as a private ledger, e.g. capital, drawings, loan accounts, etc., but this is not a true sub-division as the correct ledger in which to keep such accounts is the general ledger.

The capital and drawings accounts, although personal accounts, are maintained in the general ledger, being the proprietor's accounts in the books of the business.

The diagram illustrated below will assist in visualizing the major divisions of the ledger and classification of accounts:

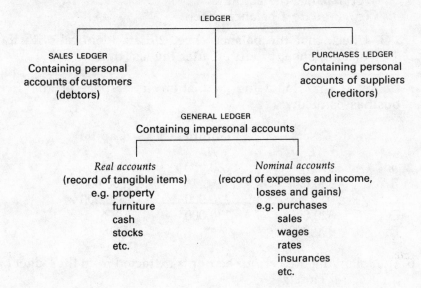

LEDGER

SALES LEDGER
Containing personal
accounts of customers
(debtors)

PURCHASES LEDGER
Containing personal
accounts of suppliers
(creditors)

GENERAL LEDGER
Containing impersonal accounts

Real accounts
(record of tangible items)
e.g. property
furniture
cash
stocks
etc.

Nominal accounts
(record of expenses and income,
losses and gains)
e.g. purchases
sales
wages
rates
insurances
etc.

Questions and problems

0–1 State the theory of double entry and explain briefly the twofold aspect of a business transaction.

0–2 Describe how the purchase of an asset, e.g. furniture, affects the financial position of a business.

0–3 State the main reasons for dividing the ledger.

0–4 Consider the following transactions of S. Silver who has £200,000 cash available with which to invest in a hotel business:

Buys hotel premises for £120,000, in cash
Buys for cash kitchen plant £20,000
Purchases furniture for cash £30,000
Purchases fittings £8,000 cash
Buys food for cash £5,000
Receives £12,500 in cash from sale of food.

You are required to:

1. Prepare balance sheets to show the financial position after each transaction.

19

2. (a) Open the relevant accounts
   (b) Record the above transactions
   (c) Balance the accounts
   (d) Prepare a balance sheet.

3. Check that the balance sheet 2(d) is identical with the balance sheet produced after the last transaction.

0–5 Complete the following tabulation in respect of the five businesses below:

	Assets	Liabilities	Capital
	£	£	£
A	310,000	60,000	*
B	900,000	*	500,000
C	*	270,000	330,000
D	820,000	130,000	*
E	990,000	*	780,000

0–6 The following are various accounts extracted from the ledger of the Kestrel Hotel:

Rent; Drawings; Sales; Capital; Fab Foods Ltd. (Supplier); Advertising; Bank; Furniture; Q. Able (Customer); Returns; Outwards; Lease; Discount Received; Wages; Loan; Insurance; Laundry; Telephone; Stock; Bank Charges; Rent Received; Repairs and Renewals.

In respect of each account you are required to state whether:

(a) you would expect to find a debit or credit balance therein;
(b) its classification is real, nominal or personal; and
(c) it records an expense, income, asset or liability.

Note: You should tabulate your answer.

Chapter One
Recording of Cash

Once the mechanics of double entry book-keeping are understood it is necessary to consider the practical aspects of recording day-to-day business transactions.

Two-column cash book

Continuing with G. Gold, on 1st January 1987 he had a cash balance of £10,000. Clearly it is undesirable to have such a large sum lying in an office. It is likely that a current account would be opened at the bank to allow cash and cheques to be paid in and drawn as required. To facilitate recording such transactions separate cash and bank accounts would normally be opened in the general ledger. However, in practice it is considered advisable to separate the cash and bank accounts from the general ledger and maintain them both in one binding, commonly named the 'cash book', this having on both debit and credit sides separate columns for cash and bank transactions on the same page (folio). By operating this method, entries recorded in the cash book will appear in one of the following forms:

Form 1
  (a) All cash received is debited in the 'cash' column of the cash book and all cheques received are debited in the 'bank' column of the cash book.
  (b) All payments made by the business are entered on the credit side of the cash book, those made by cash in the 'cash' column, and those made by cheque in the 'bank' column.

Form 2
  (a) All monies received, whether in the form of cash or cheques, are entered in the 'cash' column of the cash book on the debit side.
  (b) As for Form 1 (b) above.

Students should note that when attempting an exercise requiring a two-column cash book, with 'cash' and 'bank' columns, to be written up, Form 1 should always be adopted unless the exercise contains specific instructions to the contrary.

Where it is necessary to bank excess amounts of cash or withdraw sums of cash for use in the office then a 'contra entry' is made within the cash book alone. Double entry for the above would be completed respectively in the following manner:

Debit 'bank' column – credit 'cash' column   } Contra entries are
Debit 'cash' column – credit 'bank' column   } indicated by the
                                                           } sign ¢

The following gives information to be recorded in a two-column cash book:

On 1st January 1987 G. Gold opened a current account at his bank and paid in £9,750 leaving £250 cash in his business office. His transactions for the first week in January were as follows:

		£
Jan. 1	Purchased provisions and paid by cheque	400·00
	Paid International Stores by cheque	160·00
2	Bought provisions by cheque	1,050·00
	Cash sales	500·00
	Banked cash	230·00
3	Paid cash for postage stamps	20·00
	Purchased salamander for cash	120·00
	Received cheque from A. Parker	250·00
	Purchased provisions for cash	112·50
	Banked cash	150·00
4	Paid wages in cash	90·00
5	Purchased bar furniture and shelving by cheque	2,900·00
6	Paid by cheque for laying of car parking surface	3,000·00
	Withdrew cash from bank for office use	100·00
7	Bought flowers for cash	12·00

The transactions would be recorded in G. Gold's two-column cash book as shown in Exhibit 1–1.

Cash discounts

It is the policy of many suppliers of hotel and catering concerns to offer a discount for prompt payment or payment within a specified period of time for credit purchases. This is termed 'cash' discount. To illustrate cash discount the following transactions may be considered:

1986

Dec. 28 Purchased provisions on credit from Seafoods Ltd, £300 less 5% cash discount for payment within 28 days.

30 Sold meals on credit to F. Sands Ltd, £1,000 less 2% cash discount for settlement within one month.

31 Bought supplies on credit from MacFoods Ltd, £600 less 5% cash discount for payment within 30 days.

Exhibit 1–1

Cash Book

1987		Cash	Bank	1987		Cash	Bank
Jan. 1 Balance	b/d	250·00	9,750·00	Jan. 1 Purchases			400·00
2 Sales		500·00		International			
Cash	¢		230·00	Stores			160·00
3 A. Parker			250·00	2 Purchases			1,050·00
Cash	¢		150·00	Bank	¢	230·00	
6 Bank	¢	100·00		3 Postage		20·00	
				Kitchen			
				equipment		120·00	
				Purchases		112·50	
				Bank	¢	150·00	
				4 Wages		90·00	
				5 Furniture and			
				fittings			2,900·00
				6 Premises			3,000·00
				Cash	¢		100·00
				7 Sundries		12·00	
				Balance	c/d	115·50	2,770·00
		850·00	10,380·00			850·00	10,380·00
8 Balance	b/d	115·50	2,770·00				

If all concerned took advantage of the discounts offered, computations will be made as follows:

	Seafoods Ltd £	MacFoods Ltd £
Invoice total	300·00	600·00
Less 5% cash discount	15·00	30·00
Net amounts payable by the business	£285·00	£570·00

	F. Sands Ltd £
Bill total	1,000·00
Less 2% cash discount	20·00
Net amount payable to the business	£980·00

Recording of cash discount may be seen in Exhibit 1–2.

Exhibit 1–2

Cash Book (extract only)

1987	Discount Allowed	Cash	Bank	1987	Discount Received	Cash	Bank
Jan. 9 F. Sands Ltd	20.00		980.00	Jan. 10 Seafoods Ltd	15.00		285.00
				MacFoods Ltd	30.00		570.00

Seafoods Ltd a/c (in purchases ledger)

1987			1987		
Jan. 10	Bank	285.00	Jan. 2	Purchases	300.00
	Discount	15.00			

Discount Received a/c (in general ledger)

			1987		
			Jan. 31	Sundries	450.00

Double entry in respect of discount received is completed in the following manner:

Supplier's a/c Debit with net amount paid and discount received.

Cash book Credit 'bank' with net amount paid. Enter the discount in the discount received column and post the total of this column periodically to the credit side of the discount received account.

With regard to discount allowed double entry is completed as follows:

Customer's a/c Credit with net amount received and discount allowed.

Cash Book Debit 'bank' column with net amount received. Enter the discount in the discount allowed column and post the total of this column periodically to the debit side of the discount allowed account.

Note that discount columns in a cash book are merely for memorandum purposes and do not constitute part of the double entry book-keeping system. It is important to remember that unlike the 'cash' and 'bank' columns in the cash book the discount columns are *not balanced* but totalled. These totals are then transferred to their respective accounts.

Bank cash book

Having considered the form of cash book applicable to the smaller business, attention may now be drawn to a cash book, termed 'bank cash book', used by a larger business where all monies received, whether in cash or by cheque, are paid into the bank and all payments, other than small amounts, are paid by cheque. This in turn eliminates the need of the cash columns used in previous illustrations, replacing them with memorandum columns headed 'details'. Thus all amounts received would be entered on the debit side of the cash book in the 'details' column, and extended into the bank column when actually paid into the bank. Amounts paid by cheque are entered on the credit side of the cash book in the 'bank' column, the details column indicating the make-up of the cheque. With this system only small payments are made in cash and these are recorded in a separate book known as the 'petty cash book'.

Petty cash book

The petty cash book itself is both a subsidiary book and a ledger account. It is a subsidiary book in so much as it saves the main cash book from the burden of many detailed and insignificant entries, and it is a ledger account by virtue of the fact that it records debit and credit entries and therefore comprises part of the double entry system of book-keeping.

Petty cash is normally kept on the 'imprest' system, a term meaning 'float' or 'advance loan'. By this method the cashier is provided with a fixed sum of cash (imprest) which is used for payments of incidental (petty) expenses. The payments are recorded in a petty cash book which is balanced at regular intervals, i.e. weekly/fortnightly/monthly, to determine the total cash expenditure during the period. The cashier is then given a cheque equal to the amount of the disbursements, thus restoring the 'imprest' to its original amount.

Each payment made should be supported by a petty cash voucher authorized by a member of management. All such vouchers are numbered in consecutive order and a record is kept in the petty cash book of each voucher number. It will be evident that if checked at any particular time the amount of cash plus the value of the petty cash vouchers should equal the 'imprest'.

If the above bank cash book and petty cash book are implemented, then the following transactions will be recorded as in Exhibits 1–3 and 1–4 (see pages 27 and 28):

		£
On 1st February 1987 P. Cawson had the following:	Cash at bank	5,000.00
	Petty cash in hand	24.00

1987		£
Feb. 1	Drew cheque to restore petty cash imprest £126, pay wages £417 and for personal use £200	
	Banked sales: Accommodation £2,150	
	Food and drink £2,080	
	Purchased provisions for cash	15.00
2	Paid travelling expenses in cash	7.50
4	Paid MacFoods Ltd by cheque in settlement of an account of £2,500	2,375.00
	Purchased postage stamps for cash	4.00
6	Bought melons and paid by cheque	160.00
	Bought ballpoint pens for cash	6.00
7	Paid for lighting and heating by cheque	780.00
8	Banked sales: Accommodation £600	
	Food and drink £470	
	Drew cheque to pay wages £270 and for private use £200	
9	Purchased flowers for Room 9 – paid in cash	5.00
11	Bought by cheque furniture and fittings	1,350.00
	Paid Seafoods Ltd, in cash	50.00
12	Purchased envelopes for cash	2.50
	Purchased linen by cheque	240.00
14	Bought electric lamps for cash	18.00
	Paid Room 11's laundry bill in cash	2.00
15	Banked sales: Accommodation £630	
	Food and drink £810	
	Drew cheque to restore imprest £80, pay wages £280 and for personal use £200	

Record the foregoing transactions in suitably ruled cash and petty cash books, balancing both books on 14th February 1987.

Double entry in the petty cash book may be completed as follows:

(a) Any amounts received by the cashier are credited in the main cash book and debited in the petty cash book.

(b) All payments made and credited in the petty cash book and debited as a total to the relevant account in the ledger.

It should be clearly understood that the analysis columns within the petty cash book only serve the purpose of storing figures of similar items separately and *do not* constitute part of the double entry book-keeping system.

Visitors' paid-outs

It will be observed in Exhibit 1–4 the analysis column headed VPOs

Exhibit 1–3

Cash Book

1987	Discount Allowed	Details	Bank	1987	Discount Received	Details	Bank
Feb.				Feb.			
1 Balance b/d			5,000.00	1 Petty cash		126.00	
Sales:				Wages		417.00	
Accommodation		2,150.00		Drawings		200.00	743.00
Food and drink		2,080.00		4 MacFoods Ltd	125.00		2,375.00
8 Sales:			4,230.00	6 Purchases			160.00
Accommodation		600.00		7 Heating and lighting			780.00
Food and drink		470.00		8 Wages		270.00	
			1,070.00	Drawings		200.00	470.00
				11 Furniture and fittings			1,350.00
				12 Linen			240.00
				14 Balance c/d			4,182.00
	Nil		10,300.00		125.00		10,300.00
15 Balance b/d			4,182.00	15 Petty cash		80.00	
Sales:				Wages		280.00	
Accommodation		630.00		Drawings		200.00	560.00
Food and drink		810.00	1,440.00				

Exhibit 1–4

Petty Cash Book

Receipts £	Date	Particulars	PCV Folio	Total Payments £	Postage Stationery £	Purchases £	Travelling Expenses £	VPOs £	Sundries £	Ledger £	Ledger Folio
24.00	1987 Feb. 1	Balance	b/d								
126.00		Bank	CB15								
	2	Purchases	V21	15.00		15.00					
		Travelling ex.	V22	7.50			7.50				
	4	Postage	V23	4.00	4.00						
	6	Pens & pencils	V24	6.00					6.00		
	9	Flowers (Rm 9)	V25	5.00				5.00			
	11	Seafoods Ltd	V26	20.00						20.00	PL34
	12	Envelopes	V27	2.50	2.50						
	14	Electric lamps	V28	18.00					18.00		
		Laundry (Rm 11)	V29	2.00				2.00			
				80.00							
		Balance	c/d	70.00							
150.00				150.00	6.50	15.00	7.50	7.00	24.00	20.00	—
70.00	Feb. 15	Balance	b/d		Dr GL 20	Dr GL 12	Dr GL 21		Dr GL 22	Dr to individual suppliers' accounts in purchases ledger.	
80.00		Bank	CB19								

abbreviates the words visitors' paid-outs. This occurs when an hotel pays out money on behalf of guests during their stay, i.e. a guest may ring reception and request the hotel to obtain for him theatre tickets, flowers, or perhaps a certain book. To persistently badger the guest for such payments would cause annoyance, therefore, the value of the amount paid out by the hotel is charged to his account in the visitors' ledger

Double entry in respect of VPOs is completed in the following manner:

(a) Credit all paid-outs in the petty cash book, extending them into the analysis column headed VPOs.
(b) Debit each paid-out individually to the guest's account in the visitor's ledger.

It should be remembered that the total of the VPO column in the petty cash book remains therein.

Cash received book

It is often found advantageous for hotels to introduce a cash received book which acts as a subsidiary book to the main cash book. In this all amounts received during a day's business, whether in cash or by cheque, are recorded in the cash received book. At the end of the day this book is balanced and the total net receipts debited in the main cash book. An example of a cash received book is shown in Exhibit 1–5 below:

Exhibit 1–5

Cash Received Book

Date	Details	Folio	Discount Allowed	Total Net Receipts	Visitors' Ledger	Sales Ledger	Deposits
1987			£	£	£	£	£
Dec. 7	E. Board	RM 72		200.00			200.00
	S. Smith	RM 35		155.00	155.00		
	B. Brown	RM 58		82.50	82.50		
	G. R. Man	SL 33		97.50		97.50	
	R. Red	SL 85	100.00	800.00		900.00	
	W. White	RM 14		143.00	143.00		
	B. Blank	SL 46	50.00	400.00		450.00	
	P. Pink	RM 73		67.00	67.00		
	G. Howe	SL 50		118.00		118.00	
	Coach Tours Ltd	SL 27		117.00		117.00	
	B. Jones	SL 20		1,680.00		1,680.00	
	F. Gall	RM 62		250.00			250.00
		CB 6	150.00	4,110.00	447.50	3,362.50	450.00

Double entry in respect of the cash received book is completed as follows:

(a) The total of each analysis column (except that of discount

29

allowed) is entered in the details column of the cash book and the total of these extended into the bank column. The discount allowed total being debited in the discount allowed account in the general ledger.

(b) The corresponding credit entries are made in the following manner:

(i) Visitors' ledger column: the amounts received are credited individually in the guest's account in the visitors' ledger.

(ii) Sales ledger column: amounts received are credited in the customer's account in the sales ledger.

(iii) Deposits column: if paid on arrival are credited in the visitors' ledger on the guest's departure; if in advance and the customer is a frequent visitor, then his personal account in the sales ledger is credited. In the case of a guest who is not a regular or known customer, then a composite account termed 'advance deposits' will be credited.

(iv) Discount allowed column: the individual discounts allowed are credited in the customer's individual personal accounts in the sales ledger.

Cheques

As mentioned previously it is unwise to have large sums of money lying in an office. Most businesses open a bank account, there being two from which to choose:

1. *Current account*, which is to facilitate the drawing of cheques, no interest being received on the balance. A cheque book and paying in book are issued when a current account is opened. At regular intervals, normally monthly, a bank statement will be received, being a copy of the customer's account at the bank. A small charge is made to maintain a current account but this is insignificant by comparison with the facility received.

2. *Deposit account*, which is seldom maintained by businesses. If an account of this kind is opened, the customer is issued with a small book in which are recorded deposits, withdrawals and interest. Interest is received on the balance and no charges are incurred.

Daily, millions of cheques pass through the United Kingdom banks, giving some indication of the extent to which cheques are used. They therefore obviate the need for mammoth quantities of cash to be in constant circulation, increase control of cash and decrease the opportunity of misappropriation.

A cheque may be defined as:

'An order upon a particular banker to pay a specified sum of money to a person named or to his order, or alternatively to the bearer of the instrument.'

Banks issue bearer cheques and order cheques:

Bearer cheques: These are dangerous and seldom used. On the face are written the words 'Pay .... or Bearer'. A cheque of this kind may be cashed by the person named or the person presenting it.

Order cheques: On the face is worded 'Pay .... or Order' indicating it may be cashed only by the person named or to his order.

There are three parties to every cheque:

Drawer – the person who signs the cheque.
Drawee – the bank on whom the cheque is drawn.
Payee – the person who receives the money.

Exhibit 1–6

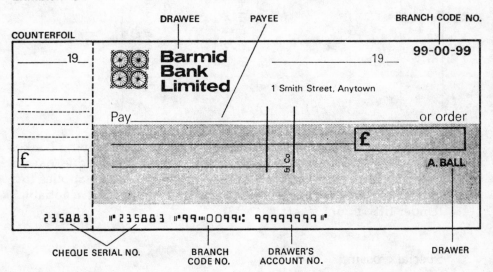

Order cheques

Endorsement

An endorsement means a signature on the back of any legal document, e.g. cheque. The Cheques Act 1957 states that endorsement is required in the following cases:

(i) When cashing a cheque except when an open cheque is made payable to 'cash'.

(ii) When passing a cheque to a third party.

(iii) Cheques payable to joint payees, if tendered for the credit of an account to which all are not parties.

A cheque may be crossed or open. An open order cheque may be cashed over the counter by the payee, or to his order.

Crossed cheques

General crossing

Where two transverse parallel lines are drawn across the face of a cheque, this constitutes a 'general crossing', with or without the words '& Co.' or 'Not negotiable'. Examples of general crossings may be seen in Exhibit 1–7.

Exhibit 1–7

The object of a general crossing is to instruct the paying banker not to offer cash over the counter but to receive the cheque, have it cleared and then credited to the payee's account. This applies to a general crossing with or without the words '& Co.', 'Not negotiable', 'Under fifty pounds', etc.

Special crossing

This consists of a general crossing with specific instructions to the paying banker, written between the parallel lines. Examples of special crossings may be seen in Exhibit 1–8.

As for general crossings the paying banker must not offer cash over the counter and in addition must comply precisely with the instructions written in the crossing. Therefore, if example 3 of the special crossings is considered it may be seen that the payee receiving the cheque with such a crossing may only present it at his own bank for credit of his own account and may not endorse it and pass to a third party.

Exhibit 1–8

1.	2.	3.	4.
National Provincial Bank Ltd	National Provincial Bank Ltd, Park Lane, London W1	National Provincial Bank Ltd, A/C Payee only	National Provincial Bank Ltd, Not negotiable

Negotiability

'Not negotiable', whether written across the face of an order or bearer cheque, merely emphasizes the position of the law and does not render the cheque intransferable to a third party. In the case of a cheque crossed 'not negotiable' the payee may endorse and pass the cheque to a third person in payment of a debt. If the third person loses or has the cheque stolen and the finder or thief offers it in payment to an innocent party then the latter does not receive a better title than that received by the finder or thief. Hence, since the finder or thief has no title to the cheque, then any subsequent transferee similarly has no legal right to it.

Note: A cheque legally remains in force for six years but banks will not accept a cheque dated more than six months before presentation; in this case the cheque is said to be 'stale'.

Traders' credits

A facility offered by banks enables one cheque to be drawn for the sum total of payments being made to creditors. The cheque, together with a list of creditors, their bankers and a breakdown of payments to be made, is sent to the drawer's bank who arranges, by means of a credit transfer system, for the creditor's accounts to be credited.

Receipt of cheques

When receiving cheques it is important to ensure the following:
1. It is not post-dated or 'stale'.
2. The name of the payee is correct.

3. The amount in words and figures coincides (this should agree with the total of the bill being paid).
4. The drawer has signed the cheque.
5. Any alterations have been signed by the drawer.

Bank reconciliation statement

On receiving a monthly statement of account from the bank, it is unlikely that the balance indicated on the statement will coincide with the balance on the same date of the 'bank' column in the cash book. There are several reasons for this discrepancy, the most common being the following:

(a) Unpresented cheques – occurring when a creditor has not presented a cheque until after the bank statement had been prepared.
(b) Amounts not credited (added) by the bank – arising when an amount of money paid in by the business had been received by the bank after preparation of the statement.
(c) Bank charges – incurred for services received by the business. These, not being known until the bank statement has been received, will not have been recorded in the cash book.
(d) Traders' credits – occurring when a debtor has paid a sum of money directly into the business bank account unbeknown to the business. This, also, will only be discovered on receipt of a bank statement.

An example of a bank reconciliation problem is illustrated below:
From the information given in Exhibit 1–9 produce a bank reconciliation statement for 31st March 1987.

Exhibit 1–9

Cash Book (extract)

1987		Bank £	1987		Chq.	Bank £
Mar. 1	Balance b/d	3,530.00	Mar. 2	Seafoods Ltd	62	430.00
7	Sales	150.00	5	Furniture	622	1,600.00
8	F. Sands	237.50	8	Bacon & Co.	623	175.00
20	R. Smithe	352.50	12	MacFoods Ltd	624	1,140.00
21	H. Jones	450.00	16	Seafoods Ltd	625	468.00
30	P.H. Motors Ltd	269.00	18	Grocer Ltd	626	832.50
31	Sales	1,176.00	26	The Dairy Co.	627	97.50

BARTINS BANK LIMITED
Park Lane, London W1
Account T. Roman

Statement of Account

1987	Particulars		Payments	Receipts	Balances OD = overdrawn
			£	£	£
Mar. 1	Opening balance				3,530.00
5		621	430.00		3,100.00
8		622	1,600.00		1,500.00
				150.00	1,650.00
11		623	175.00		1,475.00
				237.50	1,712.50
15		624	1,140.00		572.50
21		626	832.50		260.00 OD
22				352.50	92.50
				450.00	542.50
28		627	97.50		445.00
	Traders' credit			336.00	781.00
31	Charges		30.00		751.00

The problem may be solved in the following manner:
1. Check all cash book receipts against the bank statement receipts and determine the sum total of amounts not credited by the bank.
2. Check all cash book payments against the bank statement payments and determine the sum total of unpresented cheques.
3. Check bank statement for any other entries – in this case a trader's credit and bank charges appear.
4. Commence the bank reconciliation statement with the cash book balance as in Exhibit 1–10 and apply differences determined in 1, 2 and 3 above.

Exhibit 1–10

Bank Reconciliation Statement

	£	£
Balance per cash book 31.3.87		1,422.00
Add Unpresented cheque:		
Seafoods Ltd		468.00
		1,890.00
Add Credit transfer:		
Blue Coaches & Co.		336.00
		2,226.00
Deduct Amounts not credited:		
P.H. Motors Ltd	269.00	
Cash sales	1,176.00	
		1,445.00
		781.00
Deduct Bank charges		30.00
Balance per bank statement 31.3.87		751.00

Note: If the problem had been solved by commencing the bank reconciliation statement with the bank statement balance then the items *added* would have been *deducted* and vice versa.

Questions and problems

1–1 Record the following transactions in a suitably ruled cash book:

July 1	Balance at bank	4,508.00
	Balance in hand	1,881.00
	Paid rent in cash	500.00
	Withdrew cash for private use	200.00
3	Sold meals for cash	1,306.50
	Purchased fruit by cheque	117.50
4	Received cheque from B. Lawrence	160.00
	Banked sales	1,088.50
11	Sold old typewriter for cash	80.00
12	Purchased kitchen utensils by cheque	470.50
17	Paid wages in cash	317.00
21	Received cheque from M. Ainsworth	630.50
	Banked sales	2,000.00
24	Sold meals for cash	1,064.50
	Withdrew cash for personal use	400.00

28 Paid for refrigerator repairs by cheque   185.00
29 A cheque for £885.50 paid into the bank on
    21st June returned by bank marked 'Refer
    to Drawer' (account A. Walker)
30 Paid Catering Equipment Ltd by cheque   1,180.00
    Sold meals for cash   2,498.50
31 Paid wages in cash   441.50
    Banked cash   1,000.00

Balance the cash book on 14th and 28th July.

1-2 The Wordsworth Inn administers its petty cash on the imprest
system. The petty cash book's ruling for expenditure is food:
postage; VPOs; sundries. Record the following transactions in
the Inn's petty cash book:

		£
Oct 1	Cash balance	250.00
2	Chocolates for G. Field (Rm 34)	36.50
3	Cleaning materials	23.00
4	Glacé cherries	58.00
5	Registered envelopes and stamps	17.30
6	Knives sharpened	22.00
	Vinegar	10.00
7	Recorded delivery of letters	9.50
	Donation to local scouts	20.00

Balance the petty cash book and restore the cash imprest to its
original sum.

1-3 The 'Trees' Hotel operates its petty cash on the imprest system
and analyses expenditure into purchases; postage and stationery;
travelling; VPOs; sundries; ledger accounts. Bearing in mind
the above information, record the following transactions in the
hotel's petty cash book. The weekly imprest is £800.

			£
Oct 1	Cash in hand		67.00
	Cheque to restore imprest		
	Blotting paper		24.00
2	Postage stamps		87.00
3	Chef's fare to London		29.40
	Paid following accounts:		
	Poulter Bird Ltd	£72.20	
	A.F.D. & Co.	£68.40	
4	Repairs to duplicating machine		50.00
	Theatre tickets for M. Booth (Rm 145)		25.00
	Floor polish		31.60

5	Cutlet frills	12.00
	Flowers for C. Drake (Rm 21)	25.00
	Carbon paper	21.00
6	Peppercorns and garlic	11.50
7	Manager's fare to Bath	37.50

Balance the petty cash book, restore the imprest and indicate clearly how double entry is completed from this book.

1–4 On 31st August 1987 the Fairfield Restaurant received its monthly bank statement, the balance of which differed from that of the cash book at that date. On checking the details of the two records the following differences were ascertained:

Three cheques paid to creditors had not been presented for payment:

    1. National Dairies Ltd   £332.50

    2. Angus Whisky Co.   £800.50

    3. The Sunlight Laundry   £234.00

A trader's credit from J. C. Nash, entered in the bank statement, had not been recorded in the cash book – value £199.50.
Receipts totalling £1,620 paid into the bank on 31st August did not appear in the bank statement.
Bank charges amounting to £70.50 shown in the bank statement had not been recorded in the cash book.
A cheque received from R. Manning (a customer) paid into the bank was returned by the bank marked R/D, £100.
The balance indicated in the bank statement shows the restaurant to be overdrawn by £773.50.

You are required to prepare a bank reconciliation statement as on 31st August 1987 showing the balance expected in the cash book at that date.

1–5 Complete and balance the cash book set out below and then, from the balanced cash book and the bank statement which follows it, compile a bank reconciliation statement. Your answer should consist of the balanced cash book and the bank reconciliation statement.

Cash Book

		Cash £	Bank £			Cash £	Bank £
Apr. 1	Balances	130	850	Apr. 2	A. Cross		240
2	Takings	30	140		B. Spot		150
3	B. Hut	50		3	D. Scott		130
4	D. Tail		250		C. Son		210
5	S. Tate		620	5	A. Been		130

Bank Statement

		Debit £	Credit £	Balance £
Apr. 1	Balance			850
2	A. Cross	240		610
	Cheques		140	750
	B. Spot	150		600
5	C. Son	210		390
7	S. Tate		620	1,010
	Deposit interest		40	1,050
	A. Been	130		920
	£300 Loan		50	970
	Bank charges	40		930

(HCIMA)

1–6 (a) What is the effect of the addition across the face of a cheque of two parallel transverse lines?

(b) B. Brown endorses a cheque made payable to him and crossed generally, preparatory to paying it into his bank. Before he can take it to the bank it is stolen by G. Green who endorses it to W. White who takes it in good faith. Can W. White enforce payment of the cheque? Would it make any difference to the position if the cheque was crossed 'not negotiable'?

1–7 On 1st October a hotelier's bank balance was £9,168.50. From the following details write up the hotel's cash book and bring down the balance as at 7th October:

Oct. 1 Received cash £250 from J. Peterson in settlement of his account. Received from L. Temple a cheque in payment of his account, £1,750, less 2½% cash discount. Received from Hydro Engineering Co. Ltd., a cheque for £440, less 2½% cash discount.

2 Cashed cheque for wages £850 and salaries £400. Received cheque from H. Drake, £150 on account. Received a cheque from R. Davis £650, in settlement of his account.

4 Paid for new deep-freeze unit, £1,805.

5 D. Lawrence, a customer, paid his account of £500, after deducting a cash discount of £12.50.

Received cheque of £359.50 from Computers International Ltd.

F. Highfield paid his account by cheque, after deducting 2½% cash discount. The amount standing in the hotel's books was £550.

6 Paid Southern Laundry & Co., £271.50.

Sent a cheque, value £100, to Wine Shippers Ltd.

7 Received cash £5 from M. Cane.

Drew and cashed cheque for petty cash £97 and proprietor's private use £250.

Paid William Dairies £200, less 5% cash discount.

Received from P. Fletcher cash £300, on account.

Received £428.50 cash from Marks Components Ltd, after allowing a cash discount of £21.50.

Explain briefly how double entry is completed in respect of cash discounts.

1–8 The Highlands Hotel uses a cash received book in addition to the main cash book. One day's entries in respect of the former appear below:

Date: March 15th   Cash Received Book

Details	Folio	Total Receipts	Visitors' Ledger	Sales Ledger	Deposits	Restaurant	Bars
T. Holmes	Room 73	427.10	427.10				
Hanson Eng. Co.	SL60	830.80		830.80			
P. Dennison	DL14	100.00			100.00		
Luncheon	NL41	372.80				372.80	
Cocktail bar	NL42	410.00					410.00
	CB22	2,140.70	427.10	830.80	100.00	372.80	410.00

You are required to explain the double-entry to be made for each of the items bearing a folio reference, i.e. six items in all. (HCIMA)

Chapter Two
Recording of Expenditure

Expenditure may be classified under the two main headings of capital and revenue.

Revenue expenditure consists of the current expenses of operating a business, e.g. 'purchases', salaries and wages, fuel, maintenance of property and equipment, etc.

Capital expenditure comprises all expenditure incurred in acquiring assets for the purpose of earning income, or increasing the earning capacity of a business, e.g. property, equipment, furniture, cutlery, etc.

Revenue expenditure

'Purchases' is an important item of revenue expenditure and in accounting terminology may be defined as:

'All items bought by a business for the specific purpose of processing and/or displaying for sale.'

Accordingly, purchases in the hotel and catering industry constitute food, liquor, cigarettes, cigars, etc. These items, for accounting purposes, fall into two clear categories:

(a) Those bought and paid for immediately (credit cash book and debit purchases account).

(b) Those bought on credit (credit supplier personal account and debit purchases account).

In practice all transactions, other than those involving the immediate receipt or payment of cash, are recorded in a book of original (prime) entry, known as the 'journal'. This book is inadequate for all except the smallest business, as only one clerk is able to record transactions in a single book at any one time. For the medium and large concerns, the journal is divided, for convenience, into subsidiary journals (often referred to as subsidiary books) to facilitate the grouping of similar transactions and to enable more than one clerk to enter details simultaneously. It should be mentioned at this stage that the prime function of any journal or subsidiary book is to relieve the various ledgers of unnecessary and unwanted detailed entries. The diagram illustrated below will assist in visualizing the main divisions in the journal.

The general journal is maintained to record all transactions other than those entered in the subsidiary books, i.e. purchases, sales, cash, petty cash, etc.

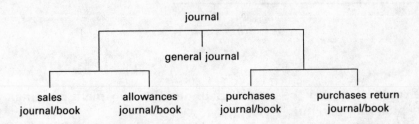

Prime documents provide the source of information for all entries made in subsidiary books and ledgers. In the case of 'purchases' this will constitute an invoice. Hence the recording of 'purchases' is illustrated below.

The following invoices, together with goods, were received by the Southdown Motel:

1987		£	1987		£
Jan. 1	Miller's Foods Ltd	270	Jan. 14	Miller's Foods Ltd	430
2	Tuff Cutts Ltd	230	25	Tuff Cutts Ltd	180
9	Miller's Foods Ltd	190	30	Tuff Cutts Ltd	200

Purchases Book   7

1987				Inv. No.	Ref.	£
Jan.	1	Miller's Foods Ltd		1	PL40	270
	2	Tuff Cutts Ltd		2	PL44	230
	9	Miller's Foods Ltd		3	PL40	190
	14	Miller's Foods Ltd		4	PL40	430
	25	Tuff Cutts Ltd		5	PL44	180
	30	Tuff Cutts Ltd		6	PL44	200
	31	Purchases Account Dr			GL10	1,500

Miller's Foods Ltd, a/c 40   Purchases Ledger

	1987		Ref.	£
	Jan. 1	Purchases	PB7	270
	9	Purchases	PB7	190
	14	Purchases	PB7	430

Tuff Cutts Ltd, a/c 44

	1987		Ref.	£
	Jan. 3	Purchases	PB7	230
	25	Purchases	PB7	180
	30	Purchases	PB7	200

Purchases a/c 10   *General Ledger*

1987	Ref.	£	
Jan. 31 Sundries	PB7	1,500	

In the above example it may be seen that all the invoices have been numbered consecutively and entered individually in the purchases book. The relevant suppliers' accounts in the purchases ledger have been credited and periodically (usually weekly or monthly) the purchases book is totalled and the total debited to the purchases account in the general ledger, completing double entry.

Note: Cross references are required to trace corresponding entries, using such abbreviations as PB, RB, GL, PL, indicating purchases book, purchases returns book, general ledger and purchases ledger respectively. The figure denotes a subsidiary book or ledger folio (page) number.

During the course of trading a supplier may be required to reduce the amount owing by a customer for one or more of the reasons listed below:

(a) damaged goods
(b) goods defective in quality   } goods returned to the supplier.
(c) wrong goods sent
(d) overcharge on invoice

Whichever reason may occur, a reduction is effected by the supplier sending a credit note to the customer. Therefore a credit note may be clearly defined as 'a document which officially reduces the value of a specific invoice'. For recording purposes these reductions are known as 'purchases returns' or 'returns outwards'.

The recording of purchases returns is illustrated below:

The following credit notes were received by the Westward Restaurant:

1987		£
Mar. 16	Meat Products Ltd	70
24	British Yeast Supplies	40
31	Meat Products Ltd	20

Purchases Returns Book 3

1987		C/N No.	Ref.	£
Mar. 16	Meat Products Ltd	1	PL43	70
24	British Yeast Supplies	2	PL45	40
31	Meat Products Ltd	3	PL43	20
	Purchases Returns Account Cr		GL11	130

Purchases Ledger

Meat Products, a/c 43

1987		Ref.	£	
Mar 16 Returns		RB3	70	
31 Returns		RB3	20	

British Yeast Supplies, a/c 45

1987		Ref.	£	
Mar 24 Returns		RB3	40	

General Ledger

Purchases Returns, a/c 11

	1987		Ref.	£
	Mar 31 Sundries		RB3	130

The credit notes are numbered consecutively and entered in the purchases returns book. The appropriate suppliers' accounts are then debited and periodically (usually weekly or monthly) the purchases returns book is totalled and the total credited in the purchases returns account, completing double entry.

Trade discount

This may be defined as 'a discount allowed for some trade purposes'. Among these may be mentioned:
  (a) An allowance by a wholesaler to a retailer, e.g. an hotel or restaurant, when goods are invoiced at retail price.
  (b) Special allowances made by manufacturers and suppliers to customers who order in bulk quantities.
  (c) Allowances made to adjust prices without the necessity of destroying existing catalogues and other sales literature.
It is important to be aware that trade discount is deducted on the invoice and *not* recorded, as in the case of cash discount, in the double entry accounting system.

Control accounts

In most businesses the largest groups of accounts are those within the purchases and sales ledgers. By maintaining control accounts these ledgers may be made completely self-balancing and independent of other sections of the accounting system.

Control accounts are often termed 'total accounts' as they contain totals of all the relevant matters relating to a particular ledger, e.g. purchases. (Sales ledger control accounts are dealt with in Chapter 4.)

This subject will be more readily understood by means of a worked example.

From the information set out below make the Robbin Hotel's purchases ledger self-balancing:

Purchases Book					Purchases Returns Book			
1986			£		1986			£
Apr.	2	A Ltd	300		Apr.	6	B & Co.	70
	4	B & Co.	200			19	A Ltd	60
	17	A Ltd	400			30	Purchases	
	25	A Ltd	100				Returns	
	30	Purchases					Account Cr	130
		Account Dr	1,000					

Cash Book

	Discount Allowed £	Bank £			Purchases Ledger £	Discount Received £	Bank £
			1985				
			Apr.	A Ltd	300	30	270
				B & Co.	250	20	230

Note that a memorandum column may be added to the cash book so that when a purchases ledger control account is prepared the amount of money paid to, and discount received from, the various suppliers may be determined by simply totalling the column.

Purchases Ledger

A Ltd a/c

1986			£	1986			£
Apr.	2	Bank	270	Apr.	1	Balance b/d	300
		Discount	30		4	Purchases	300
	19	Returns	60		17	Purchases	400
	30	Balance c/d	740		25	Purchases	100
			1,100				1,100
				May	1	Balance b/d	740

45

B & Co. a/c

1986			£	1986			£
Apr.	2	Bank	230	Apr.	1	Balance b/d	250
		Discount	20		4	Purchases	200
	6	Returns	70				
	30	Balance c/d	130				
			450				450
				May	1	Balance b/d	130

It should be noted that the entries made in the purchases ledger control account are on the same side as the entries in the personal accounts of the suppliers, the only difference being that all the figures are in totals.

Purchases Ledger Control Account

1986			£	1986			£
Apr.	30	Returns	130	Apr.	1	Balance b/d	550
		Cash paid and discount received	550		30	Purchases	1,000
		Balance c/d	870				
			1,550				1,550
				May	1	Balance b/d	870

It may be seen from the above example that the opening credit balance of £550 in the control account was arrived at by totalling the individual opening balances in the purchases ledger, i.e. A Ltd £300, and B & Co. £250. The purchases, purchases returns and cash books provided the other total figures. Therefore, as proof of arithmetical accuracy, the closing credit balance of £870 shown in the control account is represented by the sum total of the individual closing credit balances in the purchases ledger, i.e. A Ltd £740 and B & Co. £130.

In practice, having arithmetically proved the control account balance, it is of great use in the construction of a trial balance as the one particular control account figure, instead of the numerous personal account balances, may be entered in the trial balance. Hence, referring to the above example, it is more practical to omit A Ltd and B & Co. individual balances in a trial balance and simply enter the purchases ledger control account balance.

Note: The control accounts are for memorandum purposes only and therefore do not comprise part of the double entry bookkeeping system.

Advantages of control accounts

1. Errors are localized, thus saving time, labour and money in laborious checking.
2. Enable large accounting systems to be divided into separate, self-contained sections.
3. Provide a quick method of ascertaining the up-to-date amounts of debtors and creditors.
4. Responsibility for errors may be more easily pin-pointed.

Recording other revenue expenses

Having considered at some length the recording procedures of 'purchases', attention should be drawn to other items of revenue expenditure.

As for 'purchases' all other revenue expenses are represented by debit entries in their relevant accounts. The following is a sample list of the main revenue expenses incurred in the hotel and catering industry:

Accountancy and legal fees
Advertising
Depreciation of fixed assets
Heat, light and power
Insurances
Loan interest
Laundry
Purchases – food, liquor and tobacco
Rent, rates and leases
Repairs and maintenance
Salaries, wages, staff food, accommodation and/or living-out allowances
Stationery and printing
Uniforms

Double entry regarding the payment of any expense is completed by crediting the cash book and debiting the particular expenses account. However, if an invoice or bill, in respect of an expense, is received and not immediately paid, then double entry is completed by crediting the expense creditor (e.g. British Gas) and debiting the gas account.

Capital expenditure

As mentioned at the beginning of this chapter, capital expenditure comprises expenditure incurred in acquiring assets.

If, for example, furniture is bought and paid for immediately by cheque, £2,000, double entry is completed by crediting the cash book and debiting the furniture account.

If on 8th December 1985 furniture had been bought on credit from Furnishings Ltd, then, as for all credit transactions, a journal entry is required, prior to posting to the ledger accounts. Furniture is not classed as 'purchases', i.e. food, liquor, etc., therefore a record is not required in the purchases day book, but in the general journal, often referred to simply as the journal.

Due to the nature of the transactions recorded, the general journal is the only book of original entry in which both the debit and credit entries are shown.

The general journal ruling is illustrated below:

General Journal

(Date)		(Account to be debited) Dr To: (Account to be credited) Brief explanation of transaction	ref. ref.	Amount	Amount

General Journal   14

1985 Dec.	8	Furniture a/c Dr To: Furnishings Ltd a/c Being furniture bought on credit Invoice No. 42	GL5 GL49	£ 2,000	£ 2,000

The general ledger entries appear below:

General Ledger

Furniture a/c   5

1985				£	
Dec. 8	Furnishings Ltd	J14	2,000		

Furnishings Ltd a/c   49

			1985		£
			Dec. 8	Furniture	J14 2,000

Note: The personal account of Furnishings Ltd does not appear in the purchase ledger, as the firm is supplying assets not 'purchases'.

If an asset is sold for cash or on credit the recording procedure is similar in reverse. Thus in the case of selling for £80 cash an old kitchen stove, double entry is completed by crediting the kitchen plant account and debiting the cash book. If the stove had been sold on credit to R. Dobson then, through the general journal, double entry would be completed in the general ledger by debiting R. Dobson and crediting the kitchen plant account.

Questions and problems

2–1 What do you understand by
    (a) cash discount?
    (b) trade discount?

2–2 On 1st August 1987 your hotel received an invoice from Wholesalers Ltd for goods, normal retail price £500. The suppliers state that they will allow a 10% discount from the normal retail price. They also say that their terms of payment are 2½% on a monthly account.
    (a) Explain the discount which was allowed from the normal retail price.
    (b) What is the purpose of the 2½% discount which is being offered?
    (c) What will it cost to pay this account if you can take advantage of the discounts offered?

2–3 The Grange Hotel obtains its liquor from Vintners Limited. You are required to enter the following transactions in the account of Vintners Limited as it would appear in the purchases ledger of the hotel, balancing at the end of each month.

			£
May	1	Balance owing to Vintners Limited	1,431.70
	5	Bought liquor	740.30
	11	Bought liquor	842.80
	17	Paid by cheque the balance owing on 1st May, *less* 5% cash discount	
	22	Claimed for liquor broken in transit and received credit note	117.70
	28	Bought liquor	504.60
June	5	Bought liquor	285.00
	12	Paid by cheque the balance owing on 1st June, *less* 5% cash discount	
	15	Bought liquor	733.10
	21	Returned liquor (wrong type supplied) and received credit note	140.60
	22	Paid carriage on liquor returned on 21st (to be charged to Vintners Limited)	8.50

2–4 L. Davis commenced business on 1st June 1987 with a capital of

£90,000, made up of £85,000 cash at bank and £5,000 cash in hand. His transactions in the first week of June were as detailed below:

			£
June	1	Bought furniture by cheque	7,000
		Paid one quarter's rent by cheque	3,000
	2	Purchased provisions on credit from:	
		Key Supplies Ltd	600
		Shippham's Foods	450
		English Supplies	200
	3	Sold meals for cash	1,000
	5	Received credit notes from:	
		Key Supplies Ltd	100
		Shippham's Foods	50
	6	Banked surplus cash	1,000
	7	Paid by cheque Shippham's Foods, less 2½% cash discount	
		Bought provisions on credit from	
		Shippham's Foods	350
		Paid cash for stationery	170

Enter the above transactions in the appropriate subsidiary books, post to ledger and extract L. Davis's trial balance as at 7th June 1987.

2–5 On 7th January 1987 John Hanger's trial balance appeared as follows:

Trial Balance as at 7th January 1987

	£	£
Premises	10,000	
Wages	1,500	
Sales		4,000
Drawings	250	
Purchases	2,300	
Creditors		
ABC & Co.		500
XYZ & Co.		800
Cash at bank	3,950	
Cash in hand	200	
Purchases return		100
Capital		12,800
	18,200	18,200

Enter the above balances in Hanger's ledger and record the following transactions in the appropriate subsidiary books, post to ledger and extract a trial balance as at 14th January 1987.

1987			£
Jan.	7	Bought provisions on credit from:	
		EFG Ltd	1,200
		JKL Ltd	850
		Withdrew cash for personal use	250
	8	Bought provisions on credit from ABC & Co.	500
	9	Cash sales	1,500
		Received credit notes from:	
		EFG Ltd	100
		JKL Ltd	50
		XYZ & Co.	40
	11	Paid by cheque, *less* 10% cash discount, amount owing to ABC & Co. on Jan. 7th	
	12	Bought provisions on credit from:	
		ABC & Co.	400
		XYZ & Co.	700
	13	Paid by cheque XYZ & Co., *less* 5% cash discount, amount due on 1st January 1987	
	14	Paid wages in cash	1,000
		Cash purchases from JKL Ltd	200
		Bought by cheque kitchen equipment £4,000, *less* 7% trade discount	

2–6 Using the information in answer to question 2–4, construct a purchases ledger control account and prove your answer.

2–7 Below is listed the relevant detail required to construct a purchases ledger control account.

1987			
Feb.	1	Credit balances in purchases ledger	4,300
		Debit balances in purchases ledger	150
	28	Purchases	1,800
		Cash paid to suppliers	2,500
		Purchases returns	220
		Discount received	150

Having constructed the control account, you ascertain from the purchases ledger the following suppliers' credit balances:

(a) P £730
(b) Q £270
(c) R £890
(d) S £630
(e) T £160
(f) U £400

With the above balances prove the accuracy of the records.

2–8 Show the relevant journal entries for the following transactions:

1987

Dec. 14 Bought new set of banqueting tables on credit from Hotel Fittings Ltd, £15,000.

24 Purchased refrigeration unit on credit from Kitchen Supplies Ltd, £2,700.

27 Sold old chairs and tables on credit to H. Williams, £120.

30 Bought cutlery and glass on credit from Catering Equipment Ltd, £4,000, *less* 4% trade discount.

Chapter Three
Recording of Salaries and Wages

The aim of the forthcoming material is to make the reader aware of the principles and procedures involved in accounting for salaries and wages. All legislative material included is currently in force at the time of going to press, but the reader is advised to ensure familiarity with any changes the government may have since decided to implement.

The amount of money an employee earns is commonly termed 'gross pay'. From this figure there are two statutory deductions which must be made:

(a) income tax
(b) national insurance contributions.

Income tax

The method of deducting income tax is known as PAYE (Pay As You Earn) which, as the name implies, allows the employee to pay his tax as he earns his wages, rather than paying a yearly or half-yearly sum.

The amount of tax to be deducted in any one week will largely depend on the employee's earnings and his code number used in conjunction with government tax tables, issued to all employers. The weekly and monthly tax tables provided by the government (Inland Revenue) consist of two parts:

(a) Tax Table A (denoting the tax-free pay)
(b) Tax Table B (denoting the tax due on the taxable pay).

Note: Tax must be deducted or refunded in accordance with the tax tables whenever payment is made to an employee, and at the same time a deduction card must be written up (a weekly or monthly card according to how the employee is paid).

To calculate the amount of tax to be deducted from an employee's wage or salary the following procedure may be adopted:

Assume S. Hunt earns a gross weekly wage of £120. Turn to Tax Table 'A' (week 1), look up Mr Hunt's code number and ascertain his tax-free pay (say) £80. Hence his taxable pay will be £40 (£120 − £80). Next turn to Tax Table 'B' (week 1) and determine the tax due on the taxable pay by looking up £40, (say) £12. Therefore Mr Hunt's pay after deducting tax is £112 (£120 − £12).

Note: A similar method is used for employees paid monthly, using monthly tax tables.

National insurance contributions

From 6th April 1975 flat-rate and graduated contributions ceased to be payable for employees and were replaced by wholly earnings-related contributions. The contributions are now collected with income tax under the PAYE procedure (mentioned later in this chapter).

The insurance contributions must be paid by both employee and employer as indicated by reference to the National Insurance Contribution Tables A, B and C.

Gross pay (items included for tax deduction purposes)

Tax deductions must be calculated by reference to gross pay before any deductions, statutory or otherwise, are made. Examples of the items which should be included are summarized below:

Salaries Fees Bonuses Pensions Wages Overtime Commissions
Pay during sickness or other absence from work
Holiday pay
Christmas boxes in cash
Employee's liabilities borne by the employer (employee's National Insurance contributions)
Payments in respect of the cost of travelling between the employee's home and his normal place of employment
Payments for time spent in travelling
Cash payments for meals
Payments in lieu of benefits in kind (board wages, etc.)
Certain lump sum payments made on retirement or removal from employment
Gratuities paid out by the employer (service charge)
Gratuities paid out of a 'tronc'
Any of the above paid to an employee after he has left.

There are many items from which tax cannot be deducted and items which should not be included in gross pay, but these involve detail beyond the scope of this book. For more detailed reading concerning the above subjects, a list of further references may be found at the end of this chapter.

Having appreciated the basic principles involved in calculating an employee's salary or wage, it is an appropriate stage to consider the construction and layout of a wages sheet as shown in Exhibit 3–1 (see page 56).

When the wages sheet has been proved arithmetically, it is then essential that the correct breakdown of cash is requested at the bank, to enable the wage packets to be made up without running out of certain denominations of coinage. To facilitate this requirement a 'cash analysis' is prepared. Using the figures in Exhibit 3–1, the cash analysis may be drawn up as follows:

Cash Analysis

Employee's Net Pay	£10.00	£5.00	£1.00	£0.50	£0.10	£0.05
£						
179.80	170.00	5.00	4.00	0.50	0.30	–
141.05	140.00	–	1.00	–	–	0.05
115.20	110.00	5.00	–	–	0.20	–
436.05	420.00	10.00	5.00	0.50	0.50	0.05

Recording salaries and wages in the accounts

A cheque will be drawn in respect of the net wages payable (credit the cash book and debit the salaries and wages account).

The PAYE tax and national insurance contributions (employee's and employer's combined) will be recorded by debiting the salaries and wages account and crediting the PAYE tax and national insurance account.

The following illustrates the above recordings, again using the figures in Exhibit 3–1:

Cash Book

19..	£
Apr. 12 Salaries & Wages	436.05

Exhibit 3–1

Wages Sheet (week ending 12th April 19 . .)

Name	Basic Pay	Over-time	Share of Service Charge	Gross pay for week	Total pay to date	Free pay to date*	Taxable pay to date	Employee's Deductions			Net Pay	Employer's Nat. Ins.
								Income Tax†	Nat. Ins.	Total		
	£	£	£	£	£	£	£	£	£	£	£	£
Williams, R.	200.00	20.00	15.00	235.00	235.00	105.00	130.00	37.70	17.50	55.20	179.80	23.10
White, N.	150.00	25.00	14.00	189.00	189.00	76.50	112.50	32.60	15.35	47.95	141.05	21.60
Young, P.	120.00	10.00	12.00	142.00	142.00	90.35	51.65	14.95	11.85	26.80	115.20	15.70
	470.00	55.00	41.00	566.00	566.00	271.85	294.15	85.25	44.70	129.95	436.05	60.40

Note: The wages sheet should be checked for arithmetical accuracy.
* Determined by reference to Tax Table 'A'
† Determined by reference to Tax Table 'B'

General Ledger

Salaries and Wages a/c

19..			£		
Apr. 12	Bank		436.05		
	PAYE tax & Nat.				
	Ins.		190.35		

PAYE tax and National Ins. a/c*

	19..	£
	Apr. 12 Salaries & Wages	190.35

At the end of each month a cheque will be drawn for the amount outstanding in the PAYE tax and national insurance account and sent to the Inland Revenue (tax office), double entry recording being completed by crediting the cash book and debiting the PAYE tax and national insurance account.

Employees leaving and new employees

When an employee, for whom the employer holds a deduction card, leaves, a form P.45 (particulars of employee leaving) must be filled in according to the directions therein. The form comprises three parts. Parts 2 and 3 must be handed to the employee when he leaves. Part 1 must be sent to the tax office immediately. The employee should hand over Parts 2 and 3 to his new employer, who should follow the instructions in Part 2 and send Part 3 to the tax office and prepare a deduction card (weekly or monthly) as the case may be.

Payment to the Collector of Taxes

The total tax deducted, less any tax refunded, during an income tax month must be paid to the Collector of Taxes within fourteen days of the end of that month. It is sufficient to send a single remittance to include both the tax and national insurance contributions which may be due, provided a breakdown of the two amounts is clearly indicated.

Summary of end-of-year procedure

After 5th April in each year, the employer must issue a certificate of pay and tax deducted (P.60) to every employee who was in his

---

* Sometimes termed 'Collector of Taxes account'.

employment at 5th April and for whom a deduction card has been operated during the year ended 5th April. The certificate should be issued as soon as the deduction card has been completed.

The employer is required to make his annual returns to the Collector of Taxes, not later than 19th April in each year, of pay, tax deductions and national insurance contributions in respect of all employees for whom he has used a deduction card during the year ended on the previous 5th April. This is done by sending to the Collector of Taxes all the deduction cards with a covering form P.35 (Employer's Annual Declaration and Certificate).

Employers are required to keep records of each employee's earnings for a minimum of two years after the end of the income tax year in which the earnings relate.

The Wages Councils Act 1959

A large proportion of employees in the hotel and catering industry are subject to wage regulation orders made under this Act. Among their main functions wages councils have powers to submit proposals to the Secretary of State for Employment for the fixing of minimum remuneration and of holidays to be allowed to workers in relation to whom the council operates. Once the Minister has made a wage regulation order it has the force of law from the day of its coming into operation.

It is therefore of the utmost importance that employers ensure that they are offering at least the minimum wages and holidays, etc., laid down in the relevant wage regulation orders. An employer who fails to comply with these regulations is liable to fines for each offence and, in addition, must pay any arrears of wages due to the employee(s) within the last three years.

Note: For further reading list, turn to the end of this chapter.

Payroll control

Internal payroll control (IPC)

Systems in force as regards wages vary considerably with the size and nature of the business. Nevertheless, the principal features of a sound system of internal control for wages are as follows:

(a) Wherever possible the wages department should be a separate entity dealing only with wages. A number of persons should be engaged in the compilation of wage records, so that a system may be arranged preventing, for instance, one person from preparing the wages sheet *and* making up the pay packets.

(b) Employee history records should be kept containing particulars of such matters as engagement, retirement or dismissal, rate of pay and specimen signature.

(c) There should be proper procedures for checking and authorizing overtime and spreadover by persons independent of the wages department.

(d) As evidence of the work performed, payrolls should be initialled by the person responsible for their preparation and checking. Also the payroll should be initialled as approved for payment by a person independent of those responsible for its preparation and checking. The responsible official should then make out a wages cheque for the exact net amount of the payroll, the payroll again being initialled as evidence that it has been inspected by him.

(e) Wages should be paid out at fixed times and signed for by each employee personally. Procedure should be laid down as to the extent to which employees are allowed to collect wages on behalf of other employees (written authorization is more common policy).

(f) Unclaimed wages should be held by the cashier (not the wages department) and after a reasonable time unclaimed wage packets should be broken down and entered in a special bank account pending inquiry.

(g) The wages sheets should occasionally be scrutinized by the personnel officer, or in a smaller business the various heads of departments, to guard against 'dummy' workers on the payroll.

The principles of internal control listed above broadly apply to salaries. In particular there should be proper procedures for authorizing engagements, dismissals and salary increases. The precise form adopted will depend on the particular business. Regarding salaries payment, these should be made by direct transfer to the employees' bank accounts. In any event, payment by cheque is preferable to payment by cash.

Procedural control tests

In respect of salaries and wages the procedural control test incorporated in a detailed audit programme is designed to verify that:

(a) the system of IPC itself is adequate and

(b) the staff operating control procedures do so effectively.

This should ensure:

(a) employees entered on the wages sheet do, in fact, exist;

(b) employees complied with job requirement, earned the pay

indicated as payable to them and paid in accordance with rates which have been authorized;
(c) payment of salaries and wages is controlled by making sure money is paid only to the employee who has earned it.

Questions and problems

3–1 Explain briefly what you understand by the term 'statutory deductions'.

3–2 An employee paid a 'living-out' allowance by his employer will be taxed on the full amount of the allowance. Discuss this statement, giving reasons for your answer.

3–3 Explain how the PAYE system of deducting income is tax operated.

3–4 List ten items which may be included as part of 'gross pay' for tax deduction purposes.

3–5 You are required to rule up a wages sheet in suitable form in which to record the following payroll information in respect of two members of staff, showing the net amounts payable in each case:

	R. Jackson	G. Finnegan
Basic wage	120.00	140.00
Overtime	25.00	15.00
Share of service charge	35.00	18.00
Employee's NI	12.25	15.75
Employer's NI	25.10	32.10
PAYE tax	43.50	48.20

3–6 From the following net amounts payable to six employees you are required to draw up an analysis of cash required from the bank in order to make up the pay packets.

Employee A	£93.85	Employee D	£116.55
Employee B	£78.05	Employee E	£111.05
Employee C	£136.35	Employee F	£80.75

3–7 (a) The Bayview Hotel is a small establishment, and in the preparation of its payroll uses the tax deduction cards provided by the local tax office. From the information given below you are required to rule-up a wages book and to enter the details of the following two employees to show the net wage payable in each case.

E. Banks
   Basic wage £120, overtime £35.00
   Share of service charge £28.50
   Deductions: PAYE tax £25.30
                NI £17.50
   Employer's NI £24.10
 Miss H. Dunlop
   Basic wage £115, share of service charge £26.50
   Deductions: PAYE tax £32.40
                NI £15.35
                Employer's NI £28.70

(b) From the following net wage figures in respect of four employees, prepare an analysis of cash in respect of each employee, and in total, to be drawn from the bank in order to make up the pay packets:

Employee A	£97.45
Employee B	£90.80
Employee C	£118.75
Employee D	£142.05

(HCIMA)

3–8 You are presented with the following totals taken from a wages sheet:
   Total share of service charge for the week £200
   Total gross pay for the week £2,500
   Total PAYE tax deducted for the week £450
   Total deductions for the week £700
   Total employee's NI for the week £250
   Total employer's NI for the week £550
   Total net pay for the week £1,800
   Total overtime for the week £350
   Total basic pay for the week £1,950
You are required to enter the relevant information into the appropriate accounts in double entry form.

3–9 What safeguards do you consider necessary to avoid the payment of wages:
(a) to the wrong individual?
(b) to an individual not entitled to wages?
(c) at an incorrect hourly rate?

3–10 The following are the totals of a wages sheet for the week ended 15th April, 1986:

61

| Gross Pay | Deductions | | | Net Pay | Employer's NI |
	PAYE	NI	Total		
£ 9,860	£ 760	£ 220	£ 980	£ 8,880	£ 550

You are required:

(a) to post these totals to the appropriate ledger accounts and cash book;

(b) to extract a trial balance from the accounts and cash book you have completed; and

(c) to give the cost to the employer of the labour recorded in this wages sheet.

3–11 With regard to the salaries and wages department of a large business, what are the objects of implementing a procedural control test?

Further reading

Employer's Guide to Pay As You Earn.
  Issued by the Inland Revenue and obtainable from local tax offices.
Employer's Guide to National Insurance Contributions
Employer's Guide to Contracted-out Employments
  Issued by the Department of Social Security and obtainable from local DHSS offices.
Wages Regulations Orders (Hotel and Catering Industry)
  Obtainable from: 7th Floor, Hempstead House, Hemel Hempstead, Herts.

Hotel and Catering Training Board (HCTB)
  Information from: PO Box 18, Ramsey House, Central Square, Wembley, Middlesex.

Chapter Four

Recording of Income

In the hotel and catering industry income basically comprises:

(a) restaurant sales

(b) banqueting sales

(c) hotel visitor sales

(d) other income

As in the case of 'purchases', sales clearly fall into two categories.

(a) those paid for immediately
(debit cash book and credit sales account)

(b) those made on credit
(debit customer's personal account and credit sales account).

It is the second category which requires detailed consideration, viz. credit sales.

Restaurant sales

The prime document from which restaurant sales are recorded is a bill signed by the customer. Exhibit 4–1 illustrates the recording of restaurant sales.

It may be observed that the bills have been numbered consecutively and entered individually in the restaurant sales book. The particular customers' accounts in the sales ledger have been debited and periodically (usually weekly or monthly) the restaurant sales book is totalled and the total credited to the sales account in the general ledger, completing double entry.

Note: Cross reference abbreviations RB and SL indicate restaurant sales book and sales ledger respectively.

Exhibit 4–1

During the first week in September 1987 the International Restaurant made the following credit sales:

1987		£
Sept. 2	Marine Engines Ltd	90
4	R. M. Armstrong & Co.	35
5	Marine Engines Ltd	60
6	Marine Engines Ltd	70
7	R. M. Armstrong & Co.	55

Restaurant Sales Book 14

1987 Sept.			Bill No.	Ref.	£
	2	Marine Engines Ltd	1	SL62	90
	4	R. M. Armstrong & Co.	2	SL68	35
	5	Marine Engines Ltd	3	SL62	60
	6	Marine Engines Ltd	4	SL62	70
	7	R. M. Armstrong & Co.	5	SL68	55
		Sales account Cr		GL11	310

Sales Ledger

Marine Engines Ltd, a/c 62

1987			£	
Sept. 2	Sales	RB14	90	
5	Sales	RB14	60	
6	Sales	RB14	70	

R. M. Armstrong & Co., a/c 68

1987			£	
Sept. 4	Sales	RB14	35	
7	Sales	RB14	55	

General Ledger

Sales a/c 11

			1987			£
			Sept. 7 Sundries	RB14	310

Banqueting sales

The recording procedure of banqueting sales is similar to that of recording restaurant sales, i.e. the individual bills signed by the customers are recorded in the banqueting sales book (same ruling as restaurant sales book) and debited in the relevant personal accounts. Periodically (usually weekly or monthly) the banqueting sales book is totalled and the total credited to either the sales account, or a separate banqueting sales account, completing double entry. If credit is given to a customer who deals infrequently with the business then instead of opening a separate personal account in the sales ledger, his bill may be debited to a banqueting debtors account. This account, in Exhibit 4–2 below, is also maintained in the sales ledger and, as may be seen below, greatly reduces the number of unnecessary accounts otherwise required.

Exhibit 4–2

Banqueting Debtors, a/c 50

1987			£	1987			£
Jan. 4	B. R. Morley	BB2	400	Jan. 12	Bank	CB4	400
16	Iron Ore Ltd	BB2	1,200	26	Bank	CB6	1,200
27	H. Morgan	BB2	250	Feb. 2	Bank	CB7	250
Feb. 11	S. Hooper	BB3	600	17	Bank	CB9	600
21	T. Broom	BB3	350				
Mar. 2	A. Potter	BB4	800	Mar. 8	Bank	CB11	800
6	Car Sales Ltd	BB4	300				

It will be observed that when payment is received the amount is credited opposite the customer's name.

A banquet may often incorporate both cash and credit sales. For instance, a function organizer may agree to accept an account for the food, but require his guests or associates to pay individually for their own drinks. The recording is dealt with quite simply by treating the meals as normal banqueting credit sales, previously explained above, and treating all drinks sold as bar cash sales by debiting the cash book and crediting either the sales account or a separate bar sales account.

Hotel visitor sales

Hotel visitor sales is that part of an hotel's income received from guests staying (sleeping) in the establishment. The prime documents from which hotel visitor sales are recorded are duplicate vouchers, sometimes known as checks or chits, raised by the particular hotel department supplying the goods and/or service, e.g. bar, restaurant, floor service, etc.

The sales, or charges, to guests are recorded in a visitors' ledger, often referred to as a 'tabular ledger'. This ledger comprises a large loose-leaf sheet containing all the personal accounts of guests currently staying in the hotel. A new sheet is required each day.

There are two main forms of visitors' ledger, 'vertical' and 'horizontal'. If the items chargeable to guests are listed vertically, then it is termed a vertical visitors' ledger as in Exhibit 4–3.

Exhibit 4–3

Hotel Visitors' Ledger (vertical form)

Room Number	101	102	103	104	105	
Visitor's Name	Howard	Ward	Cowley	Singer	Fletcher	Total
No. of Visitors	1	2	1	1	2	
	£	£	£	£	£	£
Balances b/f	75.00	130.00		147.50	117.50	470.00
Accommodation	30.00	60.00	40.00			130.00
EM teas	1.00				2.00	3.00
Breakfasts	5.00	10.00	5.00			20.00
Luncheons		24.00		21.00		45.00
A/noon teas				4.50		4.50
Dinners	13.00	36.50				49.50
Other foods			6.00			6.00
Beverages				1.50	2.50	4.00
Wines	7.00	10.00				17.00
Spirits & Liqueurs		5.50				5.50
Beers			3.00			3.00
Minerals					4.00	4.00
Tobacco		3.00				3.00
Telephone	4.50			2.50		7.00
Laundry					8.50	8.50
Sundry charges					12.00	12.00
VPOs		18.00		10.00		28.00
TOTAL DEBITS	135.50	297.00	54.00	187.00	146.50	820.00
Cash received				137.00	146.50	283.50
Allowances			1.50			1.50
Ledger transfers		297.00		50.00		347.00
Balances c/f	135.50		52.50			188.00
TOTAL CREDITS	135.50	297.00	54.00	187.00	146.50	820.00

Conversely, if the items chargeable to guests are listed horizontally, then it is termed a horizontal visitors' ledger. Apart from actual layout, the two forms of visitors' ledgers differ little. Both comprise part of the double entry book-keeping system as follows:

Visitors' ledger (vertical form): the upper portion contains the debit side of the guests' accounts and the lower portion contains the credit side of the guests' accounts.

Visitors' ledger (horizontal form): the left-hand side contains the debit side of the guests' accounts and the right-hand side contains the credit side of the guests' accounts.

It should be noted that the extent of the charges on a visitors' ledger will primarily depend on the facilities and services offered by the particular hotel.

Exhibit 4–4

Monthly Summary Sheet

Date	Accommodation	EM teas	Breakfasts	Lunches	A/noon teas	Dinners	Other food	Beverages	Wines	Spirits & liqueurs	Beers	Minerals	Tobacco	Telephone	Laundry	Sundry charges	Total
	£	£	£	£	£	£	£	£	£	£	£	£	£	£	£	£	£
1977 Oct. 1	130.00	3.00	20.00	205.00	4.50	1,379.50	6.00	45.50	434.50	554.50	284.50	89.50	109.80	7.00	8.50	12.00	3293.80
2	167.00	12.50	17.00	184.00	11.50	659.00	2.00	57.30	371.20	701.00	183.20	34.70	90.20	13.40	6.50	6.50	2,517.00
3	185.00	8.00	21.00	214.30	36.50	1,102.00	45.00	24.10	244.10	626.50	294.10	62.60	31.80	26.00	31.40	20.40	2,972.80
4	140.00	20.00	22.50	806.00	12.00	853.40	31.70	36.20	327.60	725.40	240.90	93.60	44.90	4.40	11.90	30.50	3,401.00
etc. to the end of the month																	
TOTAL Deduct allowances	3,249.20 13.50	271.80 21.00	610.40 11.50	5,416.00 30.00	371.00 20.50	7,495.10 37.00	311.70 1.50	423.50 12.50	3,126.30 27.00	5,852.30 15.50	3,800.50 14.00	2,241.00 16.00	1,750.00 2.50	274.00 13.00	226.20 4.00	439.40 8.00	35,858.40 247.50
NET SALES	3,235.70	250.80	598.90	5,386.00	350.50	7,458.10	310.20	411.00	3,099.30	5,836.80	3,786.50	2,225.00	1,747.50	261.00	222.20	431.40	35,610.90

67

Double entry

All charges debited to the guests' personal accounts in the visitors' ledger, with the exception of VPOs, are totalled daily and entered on a monthly summary sheet (Exhibit 4–4). At the end of the month the monthly summary sheet is totalled and the individual totals are posted to the appropriate accounts in the general ledger, completing double entry (Exhibit 4–5).

Exhibit 4–5

General Ledger

Accommodation Sales a/c

			£
1987			
Oct. 31	MSS		3,235.70
Nov. 30	MSS		3,683.40
Dec. 31	MSS		5,811.60

Laundry a/c

			£
1987			
Oct. 31	MSS		222.20
Nov. 30	MSS		187.10
Dec. 31	MSS		244.30

Cash or cheques received from guests are credited in the visitors' ledger and debited in the cash book.

Allowances made to guests in respect of overcharges should be recorded in a monthly allowances sheet (Exhibit 4–6). At the end of the month the allowances sheet should be totalled and:

(a) the total debited to an allowances account in the general ledger, or

(b) deducted from the gross sales in the monthly summary sheet, as shown in Exhibit 4–4.

If the second method (b) of recording allowances is effected then an allowance account is not required in the general ledger.

Ledger transfers are normally required in the following circumstances:

(a) Where a customer has credit facilities with the hotel.

(b) If a guest defaults.

(c) When a customer has previously paid a deposit while confirming a booking.

Regarding (a) and (b), double entry is completed by crediting the visitors' ledger and debiting a personal account in the sales ledger, awaiting payment in the case of (a), and in abeyance while the defaulter is traced and all efforts are made to receive payment in the case of (b).

Item (c) requires more detailed explanation. If a deposit is

Exhibit 4-6

Monthly Allowance Sheet

Date	Accommodation	EM teas	Breakfasts	Lunches	A/noon teas	Dinners	Other food	Beverages	Wines	Spirits & liqueurs	Beers	Minerals	Tobacco	Telephone	Laundry	Sundry charges	Total
	£	£	£	£	£	£	£	£	£	£	£	£	£	£	£	£	£
1977 Oct. 1		1.50									1.00						2.50
2									15.00								15.00
3						10.00									4.00		14.00
4				5.00										7.00			12.00
etc. to the end of the month																	
TOTAL ALLOWANCES	13.50	21.00	11.50	30.00	20.50	37.00	1.50	12.50	27.00	15.50	14.00	16.00	2.50	13.00	4.00	8.00	247.50

received from an intending guest the cash book is debited and double entry may be completed by either crediting a separate personal account opened in the sales ledger, or crediting an advance deposits account in the general ledger (Exhibit 4–7).

Exhibit 4–7

General Ledger

Advance Deposits, a/c 23

1987			£	1987			£
Oct.	1	Visitors' ledger	50.00	Sept.	4	R. Singer	50.00
					9	Electrics Ltd	200.00
Sept.	28	Visitors' ledger	100.00		14	W. D. Rickson	100.00
					29	H. Mathews	150.00

Until the particular guest arrives and commences his stay, the hotel should regard any deposit as a liability, i.e. an amount owing to some other individual. Usually deposits are transferred onto the visitors' ledger, either on a guest's arrival, or when he pays his bill before departing. In either case double entry is completed by debiting the advance deposits account and crediting the guest's personal account in the visitors' ledger.

Balances carried forward apply only in the case of a guest staying in an hotel and remaining more than one night. The charges debited to his account in the visitors' ledger are totalled and the total (balance) is carried forward onto the next day's ledger. Therefore, double entry may be completed by crediting the visitors' ledger (today) and debiting the visitors' ledger (tomorrow).

Total sales on visitors' ledger

Apart from recording restaurant, banqueting and hotel visitors' sales in the manner previously described, many hotels record all their sales on the visitors' ledger, an example of which is shown in Exhibit 4–8.

Using this method, all restaurant sales, whether to residents, non-residents, or expense account customers, may be recorded in a restaurant summary book (Exhibit 4–9), sometimes referred to as a restaurant analysis book. At the end of a meal service the book is written up from copies of all the customers' bills and taken to the accounts department, ready to be recorded in the accounting system.

Double entry may be completed as follows:

    (a) The restaurant summary book analysis totals are debited under an appropriate column in the visitors' ledger, i.e. chance dinners, and credited to the various sales accounts from the monthly summary sheet.

Exhibit 4-8

Hotel Visitors' Ledger (vertical form)

Room Numbers	101	102	103	104	105	Chance Lunches	Chance Dinners	Orange Suite	Tudor Room	Total
Visitor's Name	Howard	Ward	Cowley	Singer	Fletcher					
No. of visitors	1	2	1	1	2					
	£	£	£	£	£	£	£	£	£	£
Balances b/f	75.00	130.00		147.50	117.50					470.00
Apartments	30.00	60.00	40.00							130.00
EM teas	1.00				2.00					3.00
Breakfasts	5.00	10.00	5.00	21.00						20.00
Luncheons		24.00				160.00			350.00	555.00
A/noon Tea				4.50						4.50
Dinners	13.00	36.50					330.00	650.00		1,029.50
Other food			6.00							6.00
Beverages				1.50	2.50	17.00	24.50			45.50
Wines	7.00	10.00				30.00	107.50	280.00	376.00	434.50
Spirits & liqueurs		5.50	3.00			23.00	90.00	60.00	182.00	554.50
Beers						10.00	89.50		41.50	284.50
Minerals					4.00	7.00	37.00		58.50	89.50
Tobacco		3.00		2.50		8.00	40.30			109.80
Telephone	4.50									7.00
Laundry					8.50					8.50
Sundry charges		18.00			12.00					12.00
VPOs				10.00						28.00
TOTAL DEBITS	135.50	297.00	54.00	187.00	146.50	255.00	718.80	990.00	1,008.00	3,791.80
Cash received				137.00	146.50	255.00	556.30	990.00	1,008.00	3,092.80
Allowances			1.50							1.50
Ledger transfers		297.00		50.00			162.50			509.50
Balances c/f	135.50		52.50							188.00
TOTAL CREDITS	135.50	297.00	54.00	187.00	146.50	255.00	718.80	990.00	1,008.00	3,791.80

Exhibit 4–9

Restaurant Summary Book   Dinner Service

Bill No.	Table No.	No. of covers	Food £	Beverages £	Wines £	Spirits & liqueurs £	Beers £	Minerals £	Tobacco £	Total £	Cash received £	Sales Ledger £	Sales Ledger	Visitors' Ledger £	Visitors' Ledger
1	6	4	40.00	4.50	20.00		17.00		4.30	85.80	85.80				
2	3	2	30.00	3.00		10.00	26.00	5.00		74.00		74.00	SL47		
3	11	5	70.00	4.50	30.00	32.00		12.00	19.00	167.50	167.50				
4	16	2	25.00	3.50	17.50		18.50			64.50	64.50				
5	12	3								13.00				13.00	R101
6	7	4	42.50	1.50		23.50	12.50	8.50		88.50		88.50	SL52		
7	9	4	40.00	2.50	25.00	11.50		8.00	6.00	93.00	93.00				
8	4	6	82.50	5.00	15.00	13.00	15.50	3.50	11.00	145.50	145.50				
9	8	2								52.00				52.00	R102
		32	330.00	24.50	107.50	90.00	89.50	37.00	40.30	783.80	556.30	162.50		65.00	

(b) All cash received is credited in the visitors' ledger and debited in the cash book.

(c) The total sales ledger figure is credited in the visitors' ledger and the customer's individual personal accounts in the sales ledger debited.

(d) Particulars from residents' signed bills are debited in their individual personal accounts in the visitors' ledger and credited to sales accounts from the monthly summary sheet.

Banqueting sales may be recorded in the visitors' ledger by opening an account for each banquet or function and debiting the details from the particular carbon copy of the customer's bill therein and crediting the sales account from the monthly summary sheet. If a banquet is paid for immediately, then double entry is completed by crediting the visitors' ledger and debiting the cash book. If, on the other hand, credit is allowed, then double entry may be completed by crediting the visitors' ledger and debiting either the customer's personal account or a banqueting debtor's account in the sales ledger. In the case of a large volume of banqueting, it may well be considered necessary to enter details of each bill in a banqueting sales book, previously referred to, for memorandum purposes, prior to analysing each bill on the visitors' ledger.

Where a business has a bar open to the public any sales would be debited in the visitors' ledger in a bar account, and the total posted from the monthly summary sheet to the credit of a bar sales or liquor sales account in the general ledger, the cash being credited in the visitors' ledger and debited in the cash book.

Control accounts

As explained in Chapter 2, control accounts are maintained to enable the purchases and sales ledgers to be made completely self-balancing and independent of other sections of an accounting system.

As an hotel maintains two sales ledgers, i.e. hotel visitors' ledger and sales ledger, and a restaurant only one, i.e. sales ledger, it is considered more practical to explain the self-balancing of a visitors' ledger and sales ledger separately although, in the case of an hotel, both may be combined.

Exhibit 4–10

From the information detailed below, construct a sales ledger control account for the Three Kings Restaurant, and prove your answer:

	1987	£
Nov. 1	Debit balances per sales ledger	700
30	Credit sales	2,000
	Cash received	1,900
	Discount allowed	50

Having constructed the control account you ascertain from the sales ledger the following customers' debit balances: A £150; B £225; C £75; D £300.

Sales Ledger Control Account

1987		£	1987		£
Nov. 1	Balances b/d	700	Nov. 30	Cash received	1,900
30	Sales	2,000		Discount	50
				Balances c/d	750
		2,700			2,700
Dec. 1	Balances b/d	750			

The opening debit balance of £700 was arrived at by totalling the individual debit balances in the sales ledger. The total credit sales was ascertained from either the total of a restaurant sales book or a restaurant summary book's meal-by-meal totals added together. The cash book will provide the other totals, i.e. £1,900 and £50, by means of a sales ledger memorandum column on the debit side. In this column are recorded the combined individual figures of money received and discount allowed to customers. The resulting debit balance of £750 shown in the control account is equal to the sum total of the individual debit balances in the sales ledger, as proof of arithmetical accuracy.

Exhibit 4–11

From the details set out below, prepare visitors' ledger and sales ledger control accounts for the Castle Tower Hotel.

	1987	£
Sept. 1	Debit balance per sales ledger	625
	Credit balance per sales ledger	60
	Debit balance per visitors' ledger	300
30	Credit sales per sales ledger	1,250
	Credit sales per visitors' ledger	2,500
	Discount allowed per sales ledger	75
	Cash received per sales ledger	1,150
	Cash received per visitors' ledger	2,350
	Allowances per visitors' ledger	40
	Ledger transfers	200

Visitors' Ledger Control Account

1987		£	1987		£
Sept. 1	Balances b/d	300	Sept. 30	Cash received	2,350
30	Sales	2,500		Allowances	40
				Ledger transfers	200
				Balance c/d	210
		2,800			2,800
Oct. 1	Balances b/d	210			

Sales Ledger Control Account

1987		£	1987		£
Sept. 1	Balances b/d	625	Sept. 1	Balances b/d	60
30	Sales	1,250	30	Cash received	1,150
	Ledger transfers	200		Discount	75
				Balance c/d	790
		2,075			2,075
Oct. 1	Balance b/d	790			

With the exception of one entry the sales ledger control account in Exhibit 4–11 is similar to the one shown in the previous example. It is simply the entries in the visitors' ledger control account which require explanation.

The opening debit balance (£300) was achieved by totalling the individual personal account balances in the visitors' ledger on 1st September. The sales figure (£2,500) was obtained from the monthly summary sheet. The cash received total (£2,350) was ascertained from the cash book or cash received book. The allowance figure (£40) was obtained by reference to an allowance sheet. Finally, the £200 ledger transfers shown in both control accounts must be entered as it represents individual transfers made between customers' accounts in the visitors' and sales ledgers.

Once the visitors' and/or the sales ledger control account has been arithmetically proved, the account(s) balance(s) may be used in the preparation of a trial balance, as they represent the individual personal account balances of customers in the visitors' and/or sales ledgers.

Other income

Apart from the income derived from the sale of accommodation, food, liquor, etc., many hotel and catering businesses enjoy additional revenue from leasing or renting shops or showcases around or within the establishments and also investing in other concerns, thus often receiving various amounts of 'other' income.

If, for example, a company received an income from certain business investments at the end of each quarter, then an account would be opened in the general ledger and credited accordingly, as shown in the Exhibit 4–12 below:

Exhibit 4–12

Investment Income, a/c 27

	1987			£
	Apr. 3	Bank	CB41	350
	July 2	Bank	CB69	400
	Oct. 4	Bank	CB84	300

The corresponding debit entries would appear in the cash book, completing double entry.

The recording procedure is similar to the case of a hotelier who sub-lets certain areas of his establishment. In this case a rent receivable account is maintained in the general ledger and credited with monies received and the cash book is debited.

Service charge

Many hotels and restaurants tend to make a charge for service. This normally takes the form of a fixed percentage added to charges where service has been received, i.e. accommodation, food, liquor etc., but *not* usually such items as cash bar sales or wedding cakes purchased and not produced by the business.

To record such a service charge in a hotel visitors' ledger the 'total debits' line requires to become a sub-total with a 'service charge' line beneath, representing the debit entry and followed by 'total debits'. Double entry may then be completed by crediting a service charge account, from the monthly summary sheet, at the end of each month. It is important to note that a service charge is *not* added to a guest's account until the time of his departure.

Regarding the restaurant summary book in respect of cash and expense acount customers, a separate 'service charge' column may be included in the book prior to the total column. Double entry may thus be effected in a similar manner to the other analysis totals, i.e. food, beverages, wines etc., as explained on pages 70 and 71.

Questions and problems

4–1 Why do hotels maintain two kinds of sales ledgers, i.e. hotel visitors' ledger and sales ledger?

4–2 With reference to a visitors' ledger, explain how double entry is completed in respect of the following items:
  (a) Accommodation charges (b) Advance deposits
  (c) Meal charges (d) Allowances
  (e) Receipts from guests (f) Ledger transfers

4–3 On 1st December 1986 F commenced business with leasehold property of £120,000; fittings and equipment £45,000; stocks £1,000; and cash at bank of £65,000. Calculate F's capital and enter the above balances in his ledger. F's transactions for December are detailed below:

1986

Dec.   4 Purchased goods on credit from Mark Ltd, £500.
    9 Equipment repairs £120 by cheque.
   12 Sold on credit to Spot £1,400.
      Received credit note from Mark Ltd, £40.
   15 Withdrew cash from bank for office use £1,200.
   17 Took cash for self £250.
   18 Paid Mark Ltd, amount due, by cheque, less £30 cash discount.
   20 Spot sent £400 on account, by cheque.
   24 Cash sales £800.
   25 Paid cash for goods £90.
   27 Bought goods on credit from Mark Ltd, £2,500 less trade discount of 4%.
   28 Paid staff salaries and wages £3,500.
   31 Bought new equipment on credit from Blot & Son £1,700.

Record the above transactions in the appropriate subsidiary books, post to ledger and extract a trial balance for F at 31st December 1986.

4–4 The Silver Blade Restaurant's trial balance was extracted at the close of business on 30th September 1987.

Trial Balance as at 30th September 1987

	£	£
Capital		24,130
Lenders Ltd – Loan a/c		8,000
Freehold premises	20,000	
Equipment	8,000	
Sundry debtors:		
A. Pope	250	
R. Todd	700	
G. Lewis & Co.	180	
Cash at bank	3,000	
	32,130	32,130

Open appropriate accounts in the ledger, enter the above balances therein, record the following transactions in the relevant subsidiary books and post to ledger. All receipts are banked daily and all payments are made by cheque:

1987		£
Oct. 1	Paid by cheque for provisions	180
	Proprietor drew cheque for personal use	250
2	Cash sales	1,500
4	Bought and paid for furniture by cheque	650
7	Sold meals on credit to: A. Pope	140
	G. Lewis & Co.	50
8	R. Todd paid his account, in full, by cheque	
9	Cashed cheque to pay wages	880
10	Received cheque from G. Lewis & Co. in payment of his account up to 1st October	
12	Cash sales	1,050
13	Sold meals on credit to: G. Lewis & Co.	210
	R. Todd	75
14	Received cheque from A. Pope in full payment of his outstanding balance, *less* 3% cash discount	

Extract a trial balance as at 14th October 1987.

4–5   On 1st January 1987 D. Cambridge commenced a business as a restaurateur. He opened a business banking current account with £5,000. He had a lease of premises valued at £65,000. He had borrowed £40,000 from D. Oxford to enable him to purchase the lease, and he owed him this amount. He had a stock of provisions valued at £1,020. He owed S. Light £630 for provisions. He had kitchen equipment valued at £4,700 and furniture and fittings valued at £7,800.

Calculate D. Cambridge's capital, open the necessary accounts and cash books and enter the following transactions in appropriate subsidiary books, cash book and ledger accounts:

1987

Jan. 1 Drew out £150 from bank for use in business.
    1 Bought provisions for cash £30.
    1 Bought on credit from Office Equipment Company Ltd a typewriter, £300, less trade discount 10%.
    1 Cash sales £330.
    1 Paid all cash into bank except £150.
    2 Paid insurance by cheque £200.
    2 Cash sales £410.
    2 Bought provisions from S. Light on credit £160.
    2 Accepted cheque £20 from S. Grimm for dinner provided.
    3 Cash sales £340.
    4 Sent cheque £180 to D. Oxford, interest on loan.
    4 Cash sales £280.
    5 Bought provisions on credit from D. Brown £130.
    5 Bought provisions on credit from S. Greene £190.
    5 Cash sales £230.
    5 Credit sales to D. Crockford £140.
    5 Credit sales to E. Fillet £70.
    5 Sent cheque to Office Equipment Co. Ltd less 2½% cash discount.
    5 Paid wages by cheque £170.
    5 Withdrew £100 from bank for private use.
    5 S. Grimm's cheque returned by bank. His bank account had insufficient funds in it to meet the cheque.

Extract a trial balance from the books at the close of business on 5th January, 1987.

4–6 From the following information, write up the Rockcliff Hotel's visitors' ledger and monthly summary sheet for 1st and 2nd November 1987.

Rockcliff Hotel Tariff:
    Single room and breakfast £17.50 (rooms 101–115)
    Double room and breakfast £30.00 (rooms 116–130)
    Early morning tea   £ 0.50
    Luncheon   £ 5.50
    Afternoon tea   £ 2.50
    Dinner   £ 7.00
    Coffees   £ 0.80

1987

Nov. 1 Arrivals a.m.   Room 104 Mr. F. Roberts
                         109 Rev. T. Peters
                         110 Mr. J. Morgan
                         114 Miss S. Wells
                         118 Mr. & Mrs. C. Evans
                         120 Mr. & Mrs. D. Potter
Coffees 109, 118, 120
Luncheons 104, 109, 114, 120
Chance luncheons 25 @ £5.50
Clarence Room luncheons 30 @ £6.00 (account to Imperial Sweet Company)
Arrivals p.m.   Room 102 Mrs. P. Slater
                         105 Mr. R. Wood
                         124 Capt. & Mrs. I. Smedly
                         130 Dr. & Mrs. G. Campbell
Afternoon teas 102, 104, 105, 114, 124, 130
Dinners All residents
Chance dinners 27 @ £7.00 (cash)
                 4 @ £7.00 (expense account – B. Good)
Clarence Room 40 @ £9.50 (cheque in full payment)
Telephone 102 £0.20, 105 £0.30, 114 £0.45, 124 £0.10
Laundry 102 £2.00, 110 £3.50, 130 £5.00
VPOs 118, £1.50, 120 £1.75

Nov. 2 Balances brought forward from previous day
Early morning teas All residents except 102
Breakfasts All residents
Departures a.m. 104 – received cash – account closed
                     120 – received cash – account closed
                     105 – account closed and transferred to sales ledger
Luncheons 102, 109, 114, 118, 124, 130
Chance luncheons 21 @ £5.50
Arrivals p.m. 129 – Mr & Mrs A. Warener
Departures p.m. 109 – account closed and transferred to sales ledger
                     118 – received cash – account closed
Errors discovered by control:
    Undercharged 110 £1 (laundry)
    Overcharged 118 £0.45 (VPO)
    Charged 102 for early morning tea by mistake instead of 114
Afternoon teas 102, 110, 114, 130
Dinners All residents, except 110
Chance dinners 18 @ £7.00 (cash)
Clarence Room 30 @ £8.00 (account to P. R. Simmons)
Telephone 124 £0.20, 129 £0.30, 130 £0.35
VPO 124 £0.55

4–7 (a) For what purpose are control accounts compiled?

(b) At the commencement of business on 1st January 1987 the visitors' ledger of XYZ Hotel showed a total of debts owed to the hotel of £9,780. At the close of business on 31st January 1987 the summary sheet for the month showed a total of visitors' sales as £99,240. Visitors had paid in cash during the month £18,400 and £62,240 by cheque. An amount of £7,240 had been transferred from the visitors' ledger to the individual debtors' accounts in respect of visitors who had left without paying their bills on leaving.

During the month payments in advance of £3,400 had been taken from the general ledger and transferred to the credit of the visitors' ledger.

What was the total of debts due to the hotel as shown by the visitors' ledger at the close of business on 31st January 1987?

Your answer should be in the form of a control account.

4–8 Draw up and balance off in the books of A. Host the sales ledger and purchases ledger control accounts to appear in his general ledger from the following particulars:

1986		£
Apr. 1	Debit balances in sales ledger	23,450
	Credit balances in sales ledger	130
	Debit balances in purchases ledger	810
	Credit balances in purchases ledger	14,320
30	Sales	87,650
	Purchases	21,000
	Cash received	30,010
	Discounts received	890
	Discounts allowed	1,740
	Bad debts written off	360
	Cash paid	12,500
	Sales returns	410
	Credit balances in sales ledger	80
	Debit balances in purchases ledger	Nil

4–9 (a) The Cedars Hotel uses a tabular ledger. You are required to explain how the double entry is effected in each of the following transactions:

  (i) A charge of £40 for a room.

  (ii) An allowance of £10 in respect of an overcharge on a luncheon.

  (iii) The transfer of a guest's account for £170 to a separate sales ledger.

(b) Describe the book-keeping procedure to be followed on receipt of a £50 deposit on 10th January from Mr D. Ford, until his departure from the hotel after a holiday covering the period 2nd to 16th June. (HCIMA)

4–10 The following are details in respect of the Gray Lodge Hotel:

		£
1986		
Jan. 1	Debit balances in sales ledger	2,350
	Credit balances in sales ledger	140
	Debit balances in visitors' ledger	730
31	Sales ledger sales	3,850
	Visitors' ledger sales	4,900
	Visitors' ledger allowances	110
	Sales ledger cash received	2,200
	Sales ledger discounts allowed	100
	Visitors' ledger cash received	4,370
	Transfers to sales ledger	560

Closing balances 31st January 1986:
Sales ledger   Debit balances A £1,330, B £1,470, C £920, D £690
                Credit balance E £90
Visitors' ledger Debit balances F £230, G £140, H £220

From the information above, you are required to:
(a) Construct a sales ledger control account.
(b) Construct a visitors' ledger control account.
(c) Prove the arithmetical accuracy of your answer.

4–11 Using your answer to Question 4–4, make the Silver Blade Restaurant's sales ledger self-balancing.

4–12 The following entries appear on the books of the Gateway Hotel, Oxford, for the month ended 28th February 1987. You are required to make the necessary postings into the hotel's ledger, and extract a trial balance as at that date.

Cash Book

1987		Discount	Bank	1987		Discount	Bank
Feb. 1	Capital		100,000.00	Feb. 1	Premises		70,000.00
7	Sales		2,100.00		Kitchen plant		10,000.00
14	Sales		3,000.00		Petty cash		400.00
21	Sales		1,800.00	2	Furniture &		
23	G. Sargent	12.00	218.00		fittings		13,000.00
24	K. Howard	18.60	167.40	28	Wages		1,800.00
27	Engin. Co. Ltd	90.00	1,710.00		ABC Supplies		
28	Sales		4,130.00		Ltd	120.00	1,080.00
					Catering Foods		
					Ltd	160.00	1,440.00

Purchases Day Book

1987		£
Feb. 1	ABC Supplies Ltd	1,200.00
4	Catering Foods Ltd	1,600.00
17	ABC Supplies Ltd	600.00
24	RS Foods Ltd	280.00
26	Masons Meats & Co.	1,100.00

Sales Day Book

1987		£
Feb. 6	A. Roberts	145.00
13	G. Sargent	237.30
14	H. Miller	47.00
17	K. Howard	186.00
23	Engineering Co. Ltd	1,800.00
27	Barker Press Ltd	92.50

Petty Cash Book

1987		£	1987			£
Feb. 1	Bank	400.00	Feb. 7	Stationery	47.50
			13	Sundries	17.00
			26	Sundries	33.00
			27	Postage	20.00
			28	Stationery	60.00

Allowances Book

1987		£
Feb. 14	G. Sargent	7.30
27	Barker Press Ltd	12.30

Returns Outwards

1987		£
Feb. 26	RS Foods Ltd	80.00
28	Masons Meats & Co.	100.00

Chapter Five

Value Added Tax

Value added tax (VAT) is a tax payable to HM Customs and Excise on the supplies of goods and services. 'Supplies' does not mean stocks or quantities but in fact sales, hiring and the performance of services. VAT is collected at all stages in the chain of production and distribution of goods and services, including capital goods. In the case of goods, the initial link is the raw material, e.g. food, drink, etc., and the last link is the finished item when sold to the final purchaser, i.e. consumer. Although each trader forming a link in the chain pays VAT on purchases, known as 'inputs', and charges VAT on sales, called 'outputs', it is the *final* purchaser who bears the burden of VAT.

At intervals, normally three monthly, a return has to be made to Customs and excise, and this is completed as follows:

	£
Total output tax	11,200
Total input tax	11,000
	200

Normally, as in this case, the £200 difference is payable to the Customs and Excise. If however, the input tax exceeds the output tax then the difference is refunded by the Customs and Excise.

Zero rate

Zero rating means that output tax is not chargeable on sales. However, zero-rated supplies are in fact technically taxable, though the tax rate is nil. The tax charge on inputs relating to them can be reclaimed like other input tax. Food and beverages not consumed on catering premises are zero-rated except that 'take-away' hot food and drink are at standard rate.

Exemption

As in the case of the zero rate, exemption means that no output tax is chargeable on sales. Furthermore, unless taxable supplies are also made, registration, tax records and tax returns are not required by the Customs and Excise. However, input tax charged on purchases which relate to exempt supplies are not reclaimable. It will become apparent that the only material advantage gained by an exempted trader is that he will not have to deal with the administration of VAT. Catering supplied by an educational institution to its own pupils and students is exempt, as a supply incidental to the provision of education; provided the provision of education is exempt. Supplies to staff and visitors of such institutions are taxable at the standard rate.

Hotels

Hotels for VAT purposes include motels, inns, boarding and guest houses, youth hostels, bed and breakfast establishments, residential clubs and any other establishment providing overnight lodging and catering.

VAT is chargeable at the standard rate on the full amount payable for the provision of accommodation, meals and services. When an inclusive price is quoted for a room and meals, VAT will be charged on that price and not on room and meals separately, except where stays exceed four weeks. If a service charge is included on the bill it is also subject to VAT.

Beyond a stay of four weeks VAT is only chargeable for meals, extras (e.g. drink and tobacco) and on that part of the charge for accommodation which represents the provision of 'facilities' other than the right to occupy a room. The provision of facilities is to be taken as *not less* than 20% of the amount payable for the accommodation and facilities. In situations where the amount for facilities is higher than 20% VAT is chargeable on the higher percentage. 'Facilities' in this context includes cleaning, bed making, entertainment, hotel flowers, non-personal laundry, room service, stationery, television and radio. Exhibit 5–1 is an example of the way in which this rule is applied.

Exhibit 5–1

The weekly full board terms of an hotel are £300, inclusive of accommodation and meals, but exclusive of VAT. Of this £100 is the charge for meals. The standard rate of VAT is 15%. What are the weekly terms inclusive of the first four weeks and each week thereafter?

Weekly terms for the first four weeks:
£300 + (£300 × 15/100) £345.00 per week (inc. VAT)
Weekly terms for subsequent weeks:

		£
Meals	£100 + (£100 × 15/100)	115.00
Facilities	£40 + (£40 × 15/100)	46.00
Balance of accommodation 'right of occupancy' value (£200 − £40)		160.00
Total		321.00 (inc. VAT)

The reduced (right of occupancy) value has been taken as 20%.

Where short breaks occur in stays exceeding four weeks then these are not regarded as breaks in stay and are ignored for VAT purposes. Examples include those working away from home and returning for weekends, students' vacation periods and so on. The same applies in the case of block bookings of accommodation even though a number of different people may use the rooms. Where, by agreement, certain of the rooms may be used for normal letting at particular times during continuous letting periods, this is not regarded as being a break in the continuous letting period.

The letting of rooms or halls in hotels etc. for conferences, meetings and functions is also subject to VAT at the standard rate.

Registration for VAT

A business that supplies goods and services which are not exempt and whose taxable turnover exceeds the current £20,500 per annum, must register for VAT purposes. Taxable turnover comprises the value, exclusive of VAT, of the taxable output of goods and services and must include any zero-rated outputs. In normal circumstances taxable turnover represents the total value, exclusive of VAT, of the sales to customers. However, hotels, etc. that provide accommodation to customers for periods longer than four weeks will accrue a taxable turnover which is less than total turnover. Exhibit 5–2 is an illustration of the calculation of taxable turnover for VAT purposes.

Exhibit 5–2

| | Hotel A | | Hotel B | |
	Total Turnover £	Taxable Turnover £	Total Turnover £	Taxable Turnover £
(1) Value of meals, accommodation and facilities supplied to customers staying for not more than a 4 week period	18,400	18,400	12,000	12,000
(2) Value of meals, accommodation and facilities in initial 4 week period for customers staying longer	2,400	2,400	4,000	4,000
(3) Value of meals provided to customers after initial 4 week period	800	800	1,200	1,200
(4) Value of accommodation and facilities (excluding meals) provided to customers after initial 4 week period	3,200	–	7,600	–
(5) Facilities element (20%) of (4) above liable to VAT	–	640	–	1,520
Total turnover	24,800		24,800	
Taxable turnover		22,240		18,720

Catering and take-away food

The following extract from VAT leaflet 709/2/85 (HM Customs and Excise, 1st January 1985) explains the main VAT regulations regarding catering.

'This leaflet replaces the guidance previously given in Sections I and II of the October 1982 edition of Notice 709 *VAT: Catering, hotels and holiday services* and Budget Notice 2/84 *VAT: hot food and drink*. It is in two parts:

—Part I explains which supplies of food and drink are standard-rated as catering, which includes hot take-away food and drink.
—Part II explains how you should account for VAT.

'There is a separate leaflet covering industrial catering, including catering in hospitals, schools, etc.

'If you provide overnight accommodation as well as catering, your supply of accommodation is standard-rated. You will need the VAT leaflet *Hotels and holiday accommodation*'.

'The relevant VAT liability law is reproduced at Annex A'.

'Please remember, if you need any help or advice you should contact your local VAT office. You will find the address in the local telephone directory under Customs and Excise'.

'If you are not registered for VAT you should ask for the current edition of *Should I be registered for VAT?*'

Owner and employee consumption

Food and beverages taken for personal use by an hotelier or caterer are subject to VAT at the rate in force when purchased. Therefore, zero-rated goods bear no tax, but items, such as ice cream and alcoholic drinks, which are subject to the standard rate when purchased are subsequently standard rated when taken for personal use, i.e. the VAT element is included with output tax.

Meals supplied free of charge to staff are normally regarded as having a nil value and, therefore, do not attract VAT.

Service charges, tips and gratuities

Where an hotel or restaurant includes a service charge then this is subject to VAT at the standard rate. However, a gratuity given to an individual member of staff over and above the total charge made by an hotel or catering establishment is regarded as being outside the scope of the tax.

Visitors' paid-outs

VAT is not required to be charged by an hotel on anything bought for a guest on which tax has already been charged or on which tax is not payable. For instance, if flowers have been bought for a guest at a price which included tax then the total amount will be shown separately on the bill and not subjected to tax. This is simply to avoid the guest being taxed twice. Another example which requires similar treatment to the flowers is newspapers. Exhibit 5–3 is an example of a guest's bill in respect of a week's stay:

Exhibit 5–3

	£
Guest's Bill	
Detailed bill for meals and accommodation totalling	120.00
Service charge at 10%	12.00
	132.00
VAT at 15% (current standard rate)	19.80
	151.80
Drinks in bar (at VAT inc. prices)	9.00
Flowers	3.00
Newspapers	1.00
Total amount due	164.80

Accounting for VAT

Either one VAT account or separate input and output accounts are maintained. With credit purchases, the full amount of a supplier's invoice is credited to the supplier's personal account whilst the VAT element is debited to the VAT account and the balance debited to the purchases or expense account. Where a purchases day book is used an additional column headed 'VAT' may be included, thereby facilitating the total tax for the month to be debited to the VAT account.

With credit sales the customer's bill is debited to the customer's personal account, whilst the tax is credited to the VAT account and the balance is credited to the sales account. Where a sales day book is maintained an additional VAT column may be included, thus enabling the total tax for the month to be credited to the VAT account.

The balance on the VAT account is then paid to or reclaimed from Customs and Excise at quarterly intervals. When a trial balance is extracted the VAT account is grouped with sundry creditors or sundry debtors.

VAT – not an operating cost

Except for those traders exempted from registration and whose input tax is not reclaimable, VAT is not an operating cost, i.e. like purchases, wages, etc. As stated at the outset, it is the *final* purchaser who bears the burden of VAT.

Questions and problems

5–1 In connection with value added tax distinguish between 'zero-rated' and 'exempt' supplies.

5–2 What do you understand by 'taxable turnover' in respect of value added tax?

5–3 Is it possible for an hotel's total turnover to exceed the current threshold for liability to be registered for value added tax purposes and yet have a taxable turnover below this limit? Explain.

5–4 The weekly full board terms of an hotel are £200 per person, exclusive of VAT. Of this, £80 is the charge for meals and the right of occupancy value is £40.

You have been approached by a prospective guest and asked to provide VAT inclusive weekly quotations per person in respect of:
(a) a three week stay; and
(b) a six week stay

5–5 (a) What do you understand by 'VAT output' and 'VAT input'?
(b) What is the effect of value added tax (VAT) on the profits of a
   (i) restaurant where sales (excluding VAT) are £84,000 a year?
   (ii) restaurant where sales (excluding VAT) are £56,000 a year?
   (iii) take-away catering operation where sales (excluding VAT) are £84,000 a year?
(c) Enter the following invoice into the ledger accounts of a VAT registered hotel as though it is a credit transaction:

Kitchen Supplies Ltd.	
Ranges	£1,500
VAT	225
Due to Kitchen Supplies Ltd.	£1,725

(d) What to the balances on the ledger accounts in your answer to (c) represent? In what way would they affect the revenue accounts and/or balance sheet?
(e) How are the following guests affected by VAT when staying in a VAT registered hotel?
   (i) a self-employed salesman on business in the area;

    (ii) a long-term resident;

    (iii) someone on holiday.   (HCIMA)

5–6 Using the following information and the pre-printed pro-formas (pp. 92–94):

  (a) write up the visitors' ledger for 2nd May;

  (b) make the appropriate entries in the cash received book and the cash book;

      enter the day's business in the monthly summary sheet.

        Hotel Tafiff (per person)

Apartments	10.00
Breakfast	3.00
EM tea	0.60
Lunch	5.00
Afternoon tea	1.30
Dinner	8.00

During 2nd May the business was as follows

Breakfast: All residents;

Lunch: Residents in rooms 1, 3 and 4

Mr and Mrs Greig left after lunch having paid their bill.

Afternoon tea: Residents in rooms 2, 3 and 4.

Dinner: Residents in rooms 2, 3 and 4 and Mr Richards who arrived at 6 p.m. and will occupy room 5.

Liquor: Wines for room 2 £2.30

                    "   "   " 4 £4.00

                    "   "   " 5 £2.20

Opera tickets were bought on behalf of room 2, £40

Telephone call room 2, £1.00

Apartments charged to all residents.

VAT is charged to guest's accounts only on departure and all prices quoted are exclusive of VAT. (Current rate assumed to be 15%.)

Further reading

Booklets made available by HM Customs and Excise:

Notice No. 700   *VAT: The VAT Guide* (January 1984)

VAT leaflet 701/14 *Food*

             709/1 *Industrial Catering*

             709/2 *Catering and Take-away Food*

             709/3 *Hotels and Holiday Accommodation*

Tabular Ledger

Room	1	2	3	4	5	6	7	Chance Trade	Functions	Daily Summary
Name	Greig	Rose	Watson	Gilbey						
No. of visitors	2	2	2	1						
Balances b/f	180.00	160.00	52.00	39.00						Balances b/f 431.00
Apartments										Apartments
Breakfast										Breakfast
EM Tea										EM Tea
Lunch										Lunch
Afternoon tea										Afternoon tea
Dinner										Dinner
Liquor										Liquor
Telephone										Telephone
Miscellaneous										Miscellaneous
Service charge 10%										Service Charge 10%
VAT 15%										VAT 15%
Paid out										Paid out
Cash										Cash
Ledger										Ledger
Allowances										Allowances
Balances c/f										Balances c/f

Cash Received Book

Date	Name	Rm. No. or Fol.	Visitors' Ledger Receipts	Sales Ledger Receipts	Chance Trade	Total
May 2						

Cash Book

Date	Receipts	Detail	Bank	Date	Payments	Disc. Rec'd.	Bank
May 1	Cash received:						
	Visitors' ledger	46					
	Chance	58					
2			104				

Monthly Summary Sheet

Date	Aparts.	B'fast	EM Teas	Lunch	After. Teas	Dinner	Liquor	T'phone	Misc.	Service Charge	VAT	Total
May 1	35.00	10.50	0.60	15.00	1.30	32.00	25.00	3.50		8.10	19.65	150.65
2												

Restaurant Bill Summary (Chance) Service: Dinner 2 May

Bill Nos.	Table	No. of Covers	Bill Total	Analysis				
				Food	Wines	Tobacco	Service 10%	VAT
001	2	2	13.91	9.00	2.00		1.10	1.81
002	3	4	27.19	18.00	3.50		2.15	3.54
004	5	4	22.77	18.00			1.80	2.97
006	8	3	22.77	13.50	4.50		1.80	2.97
007	6	2	11.38	9.00			0.90	1.48
Total			98.02	67.50	10.00		7.75	12.77

(Scotec OND)

Chapter Six
Trial Balance

In the introductory chapter it was explained that a trial balance is compiled by extracting all the ledger account balances, including, of course, cash books, from the ledger. Mention was also made to the effect that if double entry has been completed correctly within the ledger the trial balance totals will agree. However, even though a trial balance may agree, this only confirms the books of account are arithmetically correct. This means that, although the total debit balances equal the total credit balances from the point of view of the arithmetic, there may have been many errors made in respect of the actual recording.

Undisclosed errors

A trial balance will not disclose the following errors or omissions:
- (a) *Errors of principle*: recordings not in accordance with account principles, e.g. the purchase of office furniture debited to purchases account, instead of furniture and fittings account.
- (b) *Omission or duplication*: the complete omission or duplication of a business transaction.
- (c) *Errors of original entry*: if the amount of a transaction is entered incorrectly in a subsidiary book.
- (d) *Errors of commission*: where the wrong account is debited or credited. These errors differ from errors of principle in so much as they occur in accounts of the same class.
- (e) *Compensating errors*: two or more mistakes in the books which result in cancelling each other out.

Errors which do not affect a trial balance from agreeing may come to light in many ways. Thus, a complaint from a customer may reveal he has been charged in error for some service rendered to another customer. Errors of principle, compensating errors, etc., will most likely be detected when the business books are audited.

Where a trial balance is extracted, but fails to agree, a 'suspense account' may be opened in the general ledger and debited or credited with the amount necessary to bring the trial balance into equilibrium (there is no double entry in the ledger in respect of this entry). As each error is discovered a correcting entry is made through the general journal, often referred to as the journal, in the relevant account, double entry being completed by a corresponding entry in the suspense account. It is important to remember that an error may have been made which does not prevent the trial balance from agreeing.

Rectification of errors

If an error has been made in the books the incorrect entries should never be deleted. Instead, correcting entries should be made through the general journal and then recorded in the accounts.

Exhibit 6–1

After extracting a trial balance it was discovered that the total debit balances exceeded the total credit balances by £150.

Trial Balance (summary)

	£	£
Total debit balances	65,750	
Total credit balances		65,600
Suspense a/c		150
	65,750	65,750

This difference was carried to suspense account.

General Ledger

	£
Difference in books	150

Later the following errors were discovered:
- (a) The purchases day book had been overcast by £1,000.
- (b) A cash sale of £262.50 to G. Maxwell, correctly entered in the cash book, was posted to the credit of G. Maxwell's account in the sales ledger.
- (c) A mislaid credit note, value £30, received from Bacon & Son, had not been entered in any of the books or accounts.
- (d) A cheque for £877.50 received from A. Bridgeford & Co., was correctly credited in their personal account in the sales ledger, but the cash book debit had been omitted.

(e) The monthly total of the sales day book, £7,100, had been posted to the sales account as £7,172.50.

(f) The discount received account balance of £100 was omitted from the trial balance.

Show the journal entries necessary to correct the books and show the entries made in the suspense account.

The correct journal entries may be recorded in the following manner:

				£	£
	General Journal				14
(a)	Suspense a/c Dr	GL40		1,000.00	
	To: Purchases a/c	GL12			1,000.00
	Being purchase day book overcast				
(b)	G. Maxwell a/c Dr	SL64		262.50	
	To: Sales a/c	GL14			262.50
	Being amount wrongly credited to G. Maxwell				
(c)	Bacon Ltd Dr	PL28		30.00	
	To: Purchases returns a/c	GL13			30.00
	Being unrecorded credit note No. 148				
(d)	Bank a/c Dr	CB12		877.50	
	To: Suspense a/c	GL40			877.50
	Being cheque from A. Bridgeford not debited				
(e)	Sales a/c Dr	GL14		72.50	
	To: Suspense a/c	GL40			72.50
	Being amount wrongly debited to sales				

(f) This item does not require a journal entry as the discount received account balance of £100 is correct. The error occurred in extracting the trial balance, not within the books. All that is necessary is a debit entry in the suspense account.

The suspense account would appear in the general ledger as follows:

Suspense a/c			40
	£		£
Purchases	1,000.00	Difference in books	150.00
Discount received	100.00	Bank	877.50
		Sales	72.50
	1,100.00		1,100.00

In (b) and (c) the items do not affect the suspense account, since, although they are recording errors, arithmetically they are correct, i.e. they did not avoid the trial balance from agreeing.

A suspense account may also be used to keep items in abeyance which, owing to insufficient information, cannot be posted to their correct accounts. For example, a postal order may be received in payment of a debt. If there is no indication of the customer's identity, then the cash book would be debited and the suspense account credited. On eventually discovering the sender's identity, his personal account would be credited and the suspense account debited, therefore cancelling out the figure in abeyance.

Questions and problems

6-1 List, giving one example of each, the five errors and omissions which a trial balance will not disclose.

6-2 (a) What are the functions of the journal in the double entry system of book-keeping?
   (b) Make the journal entries necessary to record or correct the following:
      (i) An invoice for £350 in respect of provisions supplied by Wood & Sons was incorrectly posted to the account of Woodley & Co. Ltd.
      (ii) A bill for £1,700 spent on re-decorating a dining-room was posted to the premises a/c.
      (iii) A banqueting debt of £800 is to be written off following the bankruptcy of the debtor (E. Watts).
                                                            (HCIMA)

6-3 After the preparation of the trial balance of the Sandcastle Hotel the following errors were discovered:
   (a) Food to the value of £800 had been taken by the proprietor for his own private use and had not been recorded.
   (b) Some additional kitchen equipment value £600 had been debited to the purchases account.

(c) Some food stocks value £200 had been overlooked in the year-end stocktaking.

(d) A payment of £500 by a debtor had not been recorded.

You are required to state the effect of each one of the errors on the trial balance.

6–4 You are presented with a trial balance showing a difference which has been carried to suspense account. Eventually the following errors came to light:

(a) An allowance of £6.80 to a customer was entered in his account as £0.68.

(b) The total of the analysis column of the petty cash book for postage had been posted as £90 instead of £110.

(c) Kitchen equipment sold for £2,000 had been credited to the sales account.

(d) A cash sale of £70, correctly entered in the cash book, was debited in error to the sales account.

(e) Fixtures and fittings costing £187.50 had been bought and paid for by cheque but not entered through the books.

You are required to journalize the necessary correcting entries and to complete a suspense account, assuming the above errors account for the original difference in the books.

Having completed the above, state which side and by how much the trial balance was out.

6–5 From the following list of balances detailed below calculate the capital and prepare a trial balance at 31st December 1986:

	£
Finance Ltd (loan received)	10,000
Leasehold premises	65,000
Rent and rates	3,000
Kitchen equipment	4,500
Furniture and fittings	3,700
China, glass and cutlery	900
Purchases	24,000
Sales	55,000
Purchases returns	150
Allowances	50
Wages and salaries	15,000
Repairs and maintenance	430
Advertising	300
Laundry	200
Discounts received	250
Debtors	450
Creditors	200
Overdraft at bank	4,500

cont.

	£
Petty cash in hand	80
Advance deposits	100
Accountancy and legal fees	120
Administrative expenses	170

Chapter Seven

Preparation of Final Accounts

Having dealt with the basic book-keeping and accounting principles up to the trial balance, the next stage is to consider to what end the records and recording procedures are used.

All businesses, with the exception of the very smallest, will normally decide upon a regular period of time, known as the 'accounting' or 'trading' or 'financial' period, by which it may measure its own performance and progress. This measurement is basically quantified in terms of the amount of profit (or loss) made during the period. To ascertain the extent of profit (or loss) made, 'final accounts' are prepared at the end of each trading period. These comprise:

(a) Trading, profit and loss account (often referred to individually as the trading account and the profit and loss account) and form part of the double entry book-keeping system; and

(b) Balance sheet.

Construction of the trading account will indicate the amount of 'gross' profit (or loss) attained whilst construction of the profit and loss account will determine the overall 'net' profit made. The balance sheet, however, as explained in the introduction, is not an account, but shows the financial position of a business at a particular moment in time.

Prior to final accounts being prepared a trial balance is extracted to give arithmetical proof of the accounting records. This being satisfied, the nominal account balances are closed and transferred into the trading, profit and loss account, whilst the real and personal accounts are balanced and the balances brought down.

Trading account

Basically, the gross profit figure determined from a trading account may be calculated by applying the following formula:

Gross profit = Sales − Cost of goods sold

For instance, if, during the financial year ended 31st December 1986 a restaurant purchases provisions costing £5,000 and sells them all for £12,000, then the gross profit made is £7,000 (Sales £12,000 − Cost of goods sold £5,000). Thus a trading account in its simplest form will appear as in Exhibit 7–1 below:

Exhibit 7–1

Trading account for year ended 31st December 1986

	£		£
Purchases	5,000	Sales	12,000
Gross profit c/d	7,000		
	12,000		12,000

From the above trading account it may be seen that the purchases account balance was transferred by crediting the purchases account and debiting the trading account, as shown below:

General Ledger

Purchases a/c

1986		£	1986		£
Jan. 1			Dec. 31	Trading a/c	5,000
to					
Dec. 31	Sundries	5,000			
		5,000			5,000

This procedure is adopted throughout the preparation of the trading, profit and loss account.

It is clear from Exhibit 7–1 that the purchases figure represented the cost of goods sold. In practice, as demonstrated in previous chapters, provisions, etc., are often returned to suppliers and allowances sometimes made to customers. There are two methods used to deal with these items:

(a) If separate accounts are maintained for both purchases returns and allowances then they may be transferred direct to the trading account.

(b) *(i)* Purchases returns account balance may be transferred to the purchases account leaving a net purchases figure to be transferred to trading account.

(ii) Allowances may be subtracted from the monthly summary sheet prior to the totals being posted to the credit of the sales accounts or, if an allowances account is maintained,

the balance may be transferred to sales, leaving a net sales figure to be transferred to the trading account.

If method (a) is implemented the trading account will appear exactly as shown in Exhibit 7–2. In the case of implementing (b) the trading account may appear as shown in Exhibit 7–1.

Exhibit 7–2

Trading account for year ended 31st December 1986

	£	£		£	£
Purchases	90,000		Sales	200,000	
Less: Purchases			Less: Allowances	500	
returns	1,500				199,500
		88,500			
Gross profit c/d		111,000			
		199,500			199,500

According to strict double entry theory, purchases returns and allowances should be credited and debited in the trading account, but normally they are shown as deductions from purchases and sales respectively. This enables the 'cost of goods sold' figure to be shown without affecting the gross profit figure.

Stock adjustments

The other inclusion into a trading account, requiring explanation, is the opening and closing stocks.

Assume an hotelier or restaurateur commences business on 1st Janaury 1986. If his accounting period extends over one year he will prepare his final accounts annually on 31st December. Now, it is unlikely that all the business's provisions and liquors, etc., bought during the trading period would have been sold. Therefore, at the end of his accounting period he will probably have provisions and liquors left. These are known as stocks, which are duly physically counted and included in the trading account (say) £1,000 as 'closing stocks' (stocks held at the close of a trading period). A stock account will be opened in the general ledger and the entry therein will be as follows:

Stock a/c			7
1986	£	1986	£
Dec. 31 Trading a/c	1,000	Dec. 31 Balance c/d	1,000
	1,000		
1987			
Jan. 1 Balance b/d	1,000		

The closing stock counted on 31st December 1986 is debited in the stock account and credited in the trading account. This stock account, together with the other accounts, is balanced. The balance brought down then represents the 'opening stocks' for the new trading period which commences 1st January 1987.

On 31st December 1987 the opening stock of £1,000 is transferred to the trading account as shown below:

	Stock a/c				7
1986		£	1986		£
Dec. 31	Trading a/c	1,000	Dec. 31	Balance c/d	1,000
1987			1987		
Jan. 1	Balance b/d	1,000	Dec. 31	Trading a/c	1,000
Dec. 31	Trading a/c	1,200			

and again, a physical count is made of the closing stock (say) £1,200 which, as explained before, is credited in the trading account and debited in the stock account.

If a trading account was prepared on 31st December 1987 including all the items discussed, it would appear as set out in Exhibit 7–3.

Exhibit 7–3

Trading account for year ended 31st December 1987

	£	£		£	£
Opening stocks		1,000	Sales	200,000	
Purchases	90,000		Less: Allowances	500	
Less: Purchases					199,500
returns	1,500				
		88,500			
		89,500			
Less: Closing stocks		1,200			
Cost of goods sold		88,300			
Gross profit c/d		111,200			
		199,500			199,500

It will be noticed that the closing stock appears as a subtraction on the debit side of the trading account. This is normally the procedure adopted in practice for the same reasons as subtracting purchases returns and allowances in a trading account, viz. enabling a 'cost of goods sold' figure to be shown without affecting the gross profit figure.

Also, it may be observed that there has been an increase in gross profit of £200, from £111,000 in Exhibit 7–2 to £111,200 in Exhibit 7–3. This has occurred because the closing stock exceeded the opening stock by £200.

Staff meals adjustment

Staff meals are a labour cost, i.e. part of salaries and wages. As food provided for staff is not available for sale to customers, a weekly or monthly charge should be made to a staff meals account. This may be determined by making the kitchen department an allowance for food cost per day or per meal, per member of staff. According to management policy this may include full-time, part-time and casual employees. Double entry for the above may be completed by debiting staff meals account and crediting purchases account.

Journalizing closing entries

It has been emphasized in previous chapters that all entries should be recorded in the general journal or subsidiary books. Thus all nominal account balances transferred to the trading and profit and loss account should, strictly speaking, be passed through the general journal.

For example, below are the journal entries required to be made prior to preparing the trading account in Exhibit 7–3.

General Journal

1987			£	£
Dec. 31	Trading a/c Dr		91,500	
	To: Stock (1st Jan., 1987)			1,000
	Purchases			90,000
	Allowances			500
	Being transfer to trading a/c at this date			
	Sales a/c Dr		200,000	
	Purchases returns a/c		1,500	
	To: Trading a/c			201,500
	Being transfer to trading a/c at this date			
	Stock (31st Dec., 1987) Dr		1,200	
	To: Trading a/c			1,200
	Being value of stock at this date			

The same principle applies when transferring nominal accounts for the construction of the profit and loss account.

Profit and loss account

A profit and loss account is prepared to determine the 'net profit' (or loss) made by a business. Net profit may be calculated by applying the following formula:

Net profit = Gross profit + Other income − Expenses

When a trading account has been completed the gross profit is brought down to the credit side of the profit and loss account (or to the debit side if a loss).

All nominal accounts remaining after preparing the trading account are then closed and transferred into the profit and loss account. Therefore, having set the remaining expenses against gross profit and incidental income the difference will represent net profit (or loss).

A specimen profit and loss account appears in Exhibit 7–4.

Exhibit 7–4

Profit and loss account for year ended 31st December, 1987

	£		£
Salaries and wages	45,000	Gross profit b/d	111,200
Staff meals	7,000	Discount received	1,400
Heat, light and power	6,500	Rent received	3,000
Advertising	2,000		
Rates and insurances	13,500		
Repairs and maintenance	10,000		
Laundry	4,000		
Telephone	1,600		
Discount allowed	500		
Loan interest	1,500		
Accountancy fees	1,000		
Net profit – to capital	23,000		
	115,600		115,600

Note: It is important to ensure that in ascertaining the net profit for a trading period only items of income and expenditure relating to the particular period under review should be taken into account.

Treatment of profits, losses and drawings

The net profit of £23,000 representing a debit entry in the above profit and loss account is carried to the credit of the capital account. If a net loss had been incurred then the capital account would be debited and the profit and loss account credited.

The justification for these entries will be more clearly appreciated when it is realized that net profit automatically increases a proprietor's capital by the amount of such profit. The underlying reason being that the business is indebted to the proprietor in respect of capital and undrawn profits.

In the case of a business incurring a net loss, this is debited to the capital account, since it acts as a reduction of capital which has been consumed in the business.

The amounts of money and/or goods withdrawn by the proprietor during the financial period under review is indicated clearly by the debit balance in his drawings account. At the close of a trading period this balance is transferred directly to the debit of the capital account. If drawings exceed net profit (if any) the result will be a reduction in capital and, conversely, if net profit exceeds drawings then the capital will increase.

The following shows the completed capital account of a restaurateur over two years ended 31st December 1986 and 1987.

Capital a/c

1986		£	1986		£
Dec. 31 Net loss			Jan. 1	Balance b/d	200,000
	(profit & loss a/c)	3,000			
	Drawings	8,000			
	Balance c/d	189,000			
		200,000			200,000
1987			1987		
Dec. 31 Drawings		12,000	Jan. 1	Balance b/d	189,000
	Balance c/d	200,000		Net profit	
				(profit & loss a/c)	23,000
		212,000			212,000
			1988		
			Jan. 1	Balance b/d	200,000

It will be observed from the above that in the first year the capital decreased by £11,000 (loss £3,000 + drawings £8,000) and increased in the second year by £11,000 (profit £23,000 − drawings £12,000).

Balance sheet

A balance sheet is not an account but a statement which shows the financial position of a business at a particular moment in time. The reader will recall in the introductory chapter that it was explained and demonstrated how each and every transaction effects a change in the financial position of a business.

After completion of the trading, profit and loss account the remaining balances in the ledgers are listed in the balance sheet. All debit balances, representing assets, are listed on the right-hand side and all credit balances, representing liabilities, are listed on the left-hand side.

Assets are divided into two groups, viz. fixed assets and current assets. The former comprises items which are more of a permanent nature, e.g. buildings, furniture, equipment, etc., whereas the latter consists of items which are constantly changing, e.g. stocks, debtors, cash, etc.

Liabilities include capital, long-term liabilities and current liabilities. Capital may be described as a fixed liability, as it is only paid to the proprietor on termination or sale of the business. Long-term liabilities comprise liabilities of a fairly permanent nature, e.g. loans from banks or finance companies, not requiring payment for some considerable time. Current liabilities consist of outside claims on the business, e.g. creditors, bank overdraft (different from bank loan), advance deposits, etc., which should normally be paid within the trading period.

A typical balance sheet of a small business is shown in Exhibit 7–5.

Exhibit 7–5

N. Mullard, Esq., Hotelier
Balance Sheet as at 31st December 1987

	£	£		£	£
Capital			*Fixed assets*		
1st January 1987	189,000		Hotel premises	126,000	
Add: Net profit	23,000		Kitchen equipment	45,000	
			Furniture & fittings	20,000	
	212,000		Cutlery, glass, etc.	15,000	
Less: Drawings	12,000	200,000			206,000
Loan – Y. King		10,000	*Current assets*		
			Stocks	1,200	
Current liabilities			Sundry debtors	2,000	
Sundry creditors		700	Cash at bank	1,500	
					4,700
		210,700			210,700

Notice from the above balance sheet that the assets and liabilities are listed in order of permanency. Also, it will be observed that a breakdown of the capital account is shown, not merely the balance on 31st December 1987.

Attention should finally be drawn to the headings applying to the final accounts and balance sheet. Trading, profit and loss account, whether shown together as one account or separately, should be worded:

Trading, profit and loss account for the .... ended ....
Whereas the balance sheet should be worded:

Balance sheet as at ....
Clearly the former relates to the complete period under review, whereas the latter relates to a particular moment in time.

Exhibit 7–6 illustrates the preparation of a set of final accounts from the following trial balance.

Trial Balance as at 30th June 1987

	£	£
Capital		239,000
Freehold premises	200,000	
Kitchen plant	20,000	
Furniture and fittings	30,000	
Purchases	40,700	
Sales		110,000
Returns outwards		400
Allowances	250	
Salaries and wages	30,000	
Repairs and renewals	2,700	
Bank charges	150	
Insurances	800	
Drawings	17,000	
Telephone	1,600	
Sundry debtors	1,000	
Sundry creditors		850
Rates	2,400	
Discount allowed	50	
Discount received		750
Stationery	350	
Cash at bank	3,500	
Cash in hand	500	
	351,000	351,000

Exhibit 7–6

Trading, Profit and Loss Account for year ended 30th June 1987

	£	£		£	£
Purchases	40,700		Sales	110,000	
Less: Returns outwards	400		*Less:* Allowances	250	
					109,750
Cost of goods sold		40,300			
Gross profit c/d		69,450			
		109,750			109,750
Salaries & wages		30,000	Gross profit b/d		69,450
Rates		2,400	Discount received		750
Insurances		800			
Repairs & renewals		2,700			
Telephone		1,600			
Discount allowed		50			
Stationery		350			
Bank charges		150			
Net profit – to capital		32,150			
		70,200			70,200

Balance Sheet as at 30th June 1987

	£	£		£	£
Capital	239,000		*Fixed assets*		
Add: Net profit	32,150		Freehold premises	200,000	
			Kitchen plant	20,000	
	271,150		Furniture & fittings	30,000	
Less: Drawings	17,000				250,000
		254,150			
			Current assets		
Current liabilities			Sundry debtors	1,000	
Sundry creditors		850	Cash at bank	3,500	
			Cash in hand	500	
					5,000
		255,000			255,000

It will be noted that there are no opening or closing stocks. Any stocks at the year end, i.e. closing stocks would have had the effect of increasing current assets and increasing by the same amount gross profit, net profit and capital.

Vertical presentation of final accounts

For many years final accounts have been presented in ledger form (as above). However, the tendency today is to abandon the two-sided approach, and to present the information in a vertical manner.

Those who are unaccustomed to the traditional system of debits and credits are able to understand the modern vertical form far more easily.

Below is an example showing the layout of vertical accounts using the information in Exhibits 7–3, 7–4 and 7–5.

Trading, Profit and Loss Account for year ended 31st December 1988

	£	£	£
Sales (net)			199,500
Less: Cost of goods sold			
Opening stock	1,000		
Purchases (net)	88,500		
		89,500	
Less: Closing stock		1,200	
			88,300
GROSS PROFIT			111,200
Add: Discount received	1,400		
Rent received	3,000		
			4,400
			115,600
Less: Overheads			
Salaries and wages		45,000	
Staff meals		7,000	
Heat, light and power		6,500	
Advertising		2,000	
Rates and insurances		13,500	
Repairs and maintenance		10,000	
Laundry		4,000	
Telephone		1,600	
Discount allowed		500	
Loan interest		1,500	
Accounting fees		1,000	
			92,600
NET PROFIT			23,000

Balance Sheet as at 31st December, 1987

FIXED ASSETS	£	£	£
Hotel premises		126,000	
Kitchen equipment		45,000	
Furniture and fittings		20,000	
China, glass, etc.		15,000	
			206,000
CURRENT ASSETS			
Stocks	1,200		
Sundry debtors	2,000		
Cash at bank	1,500		
		4,700	
Less: CURRENT LIABILITIES			
Sundry creditors		700	
WORKING CAPITAL			4,000
			210,000
REPRESENTED BY:			
CAPITAL		£	£
1.1.87		189,000	
Add: Net profit		23,000	
		212,000	
Less: Drawings		12,000	
			200,000
Loan – Y. King			10,000
			210,000

Note: (a) The figure of £4,000 (£4,700 − £700) represents the 'working capital' of the business.

(b) The 'capital employed' figure may be calculated as:

(i) Fixed assets + Working capital; or

(ii) Capital + Long-term liabilities.

Questions and problems

7–1 Explain the object of preparing a trading, profit and loss account and balance sheet.

7–2 Show the journal entries necessary to transfer the following balances to the trading, profit and loss account at 31st December 1986:

	£
Purchases	34,000
Sales	80,000
Closing stock	5,000
Salaries and wages	24,000
Insurances	1,000

7–3 Explain what you understand by:
   (a) long-term liabilities
   (b) current liabilities
   (c) fixed assets
   (d) current assets.

7–4 From the following information you are required to prepare a trading, profit and loss account for the year ended 31st December and a balance sheet as at that date:

	£
Sales	50,000
Cost of goods sold	20,000
Wages	12,000
Other expenses	8,000
Fixed assets	100,000
Current assets	3,000
Current liabilities	2,000
Long-term liabilities	35,000
Owner's capital	56,000

Presentation is important.

7–5 The following trial balance was extracted from the books of the Unicorn Hotel on 31st July 1987.

	£	£
Capital		309,000
Leasehold premises	250,000	
Furniture and fixtures	80,000	
Stock 1st August 1976	4,000	
Purchases	36,000	
Sales		90,000
Salaries and wages	33,000	
Discount allowed	200	
Postage and telephone	800	
Gas and electricity	1,500	
Debtors	3,000	
Creditors		2,000
Bank overdraft		8,000
Cash in hand	500	
	409,000	409,000

You are required to prepare the hotel's trading, profit and loss

113

account for the year ended 31st July 1987, and a balance sheet as at that date. Stocks at 31st July 1987 were valued at £5,000.

7–6 From the following trial balance prepare the Southsea Restaurant's final accounts for the year ended 30th November, 1986, and balance sheet as at that date.

	£	£
Capital		40,000
Furniture and fittings	10,000	
Kitchen equipment	5,000	
China, glass and cutlery	2,500	
Drawings	2,000	
Stocks 1st December 1985	700	
Purchases	17,000	
Returns outwards		150
Sales		22,000
Staff meals	600	
Rent and rates	4,000	
Salaries and wages	13,800	
Heat, light and power	1,100	
Printing and stationery	250	
Legal fees	200	
Loan – D. Rich		2,000
Debtors	750	
Creditors		600
Cash at bank	7,205	
Petty cash in hand	30	
Rent received		400
Discount allowed	80	
Discount received		65
	65,215	65,215

Stock at 30th November 1986 valued at £800.

7–7

	A £	B £	C £	D £
Owner's capital	30,000	50,000	*	60,000
Kitchen plant	20,000	10,000	60,000	Nil
Cash	1,000	2,000	Nil	4,000
Loan	20,000	Nil	Nil	10,000
Stock	4,000	20,000	40,000	*
Premises	25,000	60,000	20,000	Nil
Debtors	13,000	30,000	10,000	9,000
Creditors	*	10,000	30,000	20,000
Bank overdraft	7,100	Nil	15,000	2,200
Net profit	2,100	*	40,000	1,000

Rearrange the items into balance sheet form, insert the missing figures and calculate the working capital in each case.

Chapter Eight

Accounting Adjustments –
Routine and Year End

As previously mentioned, an important object in maintaining an adequate accounting system is to enable the proprietor of a business to calculate accurately his trading result at the end of each accounting period. In order to ascertain the results of a business accurately it is essential that the total expenditure incurred (whether actually paid or not) and total losses sustained (whether actually known or simply estimated) during the period in question should be charged against profits in the profit and loss account for that period. Similarly, income or gains for the period (whether actually received or not) should be credited in the profit and loss account for the period under review.

From a practical standpoint it will be appreciated that at the end of a financial period certain expenses will have been incurred but not recorded in the accounts. Conversely, income due in the period may not have been received and therefore not recorded. There is also the possibility that payments may have been made for items of expense which are of partial benefit to a subsequent period. Thus it becomes apparent that certain end-of-period adjustments must be made in the accounts before transfer to the profit and loss account, to enable true totals of income and expenditure to be achieved for that period under review.

Prepayments and accrued expenses

Prepayments are payments made in one period which relate partially to a subsequent period. Accrued expenses refer to expenses which have built up during a trading period but have not been paid by the end of that period.

Prepayments

The financial year of the A.B. Cafe Company runs annually from 1st January to 31st December. On 1st May 1986 the company took out a contents insurance policy. The premium was £360 per annum, payable in advance. Write up the insurance account in the company's ledger, balance the account at the end of the period and show the relevant profit and loss account and balance sheet extracts.

The annual premium of £360 is paid and recorded by crediting the cash book and debiting the insurance account. At the end of the period the profit and loss account charge is calculated on the basis that eight months' insurance cover has been enjoyed, amounting to £240, thus being a fair charge against profits, double entry having been completed by crediting the insurance account and debiting the profit and loss account. The remaining debit balance of £120 on the insurance account is listed in the balance sheet under current assets. This amount will be charged against the 1987 profit together with two-thirds of the new payment made on 1st May 1987. Thus, the insurance charge will amount to £360 (£120–1st Jan to 30th April + £240–1st May to 31st December).

General Ledger

Insurance Account

1986		£	1986		£
May 1	Bank	360	Dec. 31	Profit & loss a/c	240
				Balance c/d	120
		360			360
1987					
Jan. 1	Balance b/d	120			

Profit and Loss Account (extract) for year ended 31st Dec. 1986		Balance Sheet (extract) as at 31st Dec. 1986	
	£		£
Insurance	240	*Current assets* Prepaid insurance	120

Accrued expenses

The accounting period of the P.Q. Motel runs annually from 1st July to 30th June. During 1986 and 1987 the following gas bills were paid:

2nd October 1986	£1,850	7th January 1987	£900
4th April 1987	£1,200	3rd July 1987	£1,650

Record the payments in the gas account in the business's ledger, balance the account at the end of the period and show relevant profit and loss account and balance sheet extracts.

General ledger

Gas Account

1986			£			£
Oct. 2	Bank	1,850		June 30 Profit & loss a/c	5,600
1987						
Jan. 7	Bank	900			
Apr. 4	Bank	1,200			
June 30	Balance c/d	1,650			
		5,600			5,600
July 3	Bank	1,650		July 1 Balance b/d	1,650

Profit and Loss Account (extract) for year ended 30th June 1987		Balance Sheet (extract) as at 30th June 1987	
	£		£
Gas	5,600	*Current liabilities* Accrued gas 1,650	

The individual payments are effected by crediting the cash book and debiting the gas account. At the end of the period the profit and loss account charge is calculated at £5,600, as that is the total value of gas used in the period. The remaining credit balance on the gas account of £1,650 will be listed in the balance sheet under current liabilities. The final payment made on 3rd July 1987 discharges the amount outstanding on 30th June 1987.

Note: All the above adjusting entries, together with all other adjusting entries, should first be passed through the journal prior to posting to the ledger accounts.

Bad debts

A debt is proclaimed 'bad' when all reasonable efforts to recover the money have failed.

Bad debts may fundamentally be separated into three categories: those debts written off, recovered, and provided for.

Bad debts written off

If a customer's personal account balance, i.e. his debt, is proclaimed irrecoverable then it is not prudent accounting practice to allow such a debt to remain in the sales ledger of a business signifying itself to be an asset. The policy adopted should be one of 'writing off' the debt. This is effected by crediting the customer's account in

117

the sales ledger and debiting a bad debts account in the general ledger, thus transferring an asset value to an expense account. At the end of the accounting period the balance on the bad debts account may be transferred to the profit and loss account where it will appear on the debit as a charge against profits.

Bad debts recovered

Occasionally a debt which has been written off as bad in a current or previous period may later be realized. In the event of this occurring the recording may be effected by debiting the cash book and crediting a bad debts recovered account in the general ledger. Again, at the end of the period, the balance on the bad debts recovered account may be transferred to the profit and loss account, in this case appearing on the credit as an income.

Bad debts provisions

In addition to writing off bad debts it is considered important to provide against the possibility of debts likely to become irrecoverable. Basically there are three methods of determining the extent of the estimated provision to be made:

1. To decide on a percentage, based on past records and experience, of the total debtors at the end of a trading period.
2. To provide for specific debts considered likely to become irrecoverable.
3. A combination of methods 1 and 2.

Method 1 is the more usual choice in practice.

Exhibit 8–1 demonstrates the accounting treatment of providing for bad and doubtful debts.

Exhibit 8–1

It is the policy of the L.M. Hotel, at the end of each accounting period, to provide 4% for doubtful debts on total debtors. At 31st December 1985 and 1986, debtors totalled £5,000 and £6,500 respectively. Record the provision in the hotel's provision for doubtful debts account and show the relevant profit and loss account and balance sheet extracts.

In the first year (ended 31st December 1985) double entry was effected by crediting the provision for doubtful debts account £200 and debiting the profit and loss account £200. The provision for doubtful debts balance is later entered in the balance sheet, not on

Provision for Doubtful Debts Account

1985		£	1985		£
Dec. 31	Balance c/d (4% of £5,000)	200	Dec. 31	Profit and loss a/c	200
1986			1986		
Dec. 31	Balance c/d (4% of £6,500)	260	Jan. 1	Balance b/d	200
			Dec. 31	Profit and loss a/c	60
		260			260
			1987		
			Jan. 1	Balance b/d	260

Profit and Loss Account (extract)
for year ended 31st Dec. 1985

	£	
Provn. for bad debts	200	

Balance Sheet (extract)
as at 31st Dec. 1985

		£	£
Current assets			
Debtors		5,000	
Less: Provn. for bad debts		200	
			4,800

Profit and Loss Account (extract)
for year ended 31st Dec. 1986

	£	
Provn. for bad debts	60	

Balance Sheet (extract)
as at 31st Dec. 1986

		£	£
Current assets			
Debtors		6,500	
Less: Provn. for bad debts		260	
			6,240

the liabilities side, but on the assets side as a deduction from debtors, and so showing a more realistic value of the debtors' figure. In the second year (ended 31st December 1986) a provision for doubtful debts of £260 is required, but it will be observed that in the ledger the provision for doubtful debts account already has a balance of £200, therefore only the difference need be added by crediting the provision for doubtful debts account £60 and debiting the profit and loss account £60.

Note: Once a provision for doubtful debts has been established the only adjustment required in subsequent periods is an increase (as in the above example) or a decrease, according to the extent of the percentage to total debtors at the end of a period.

The above procedure of recording bad debts requires three entries to be made in the profit and loss account, viz. bad debts written off, bad debts recovered and bad debts provision. An alternative method for treating bad debts, used quite frequently, is to maintain three separate ledger accounts as before but at the end of the financial period to transfer the bad debts written off and bad debts recovered account balances to the provision for doubtful debts account, so enabling just one figure of bad debts (net) to be posted to the profit and loss account thus assisting in reducing the number of entries therein.

If this method were implemented then the provision for doubtful debts account (for year ended 31st December 1985) in Exhibit 8–2 would be as in Exhibit 8–3.

Exhibit 8–2

Provision for Doubtful Debts Account

1985		£	1985		£
Dec. 31	Bad debts w/o	180	Dec. 31	Bad debts (recovered)	40
	Balance c/d			Profit & Loss a/c	340
	(4% of £5,000)	200			
		380			380
			1986		
			Jan. 1	Balance b/d	200

Profit and Loss Account (extract) for year ended 31st Dec. 1985			Balance Sheet (extract) as at 31st Dec. 1985		
	£			£	£
Bad debts	340		*Current assets*		
			Debtors	5,000	
			Less: Provn.		
			for bad debts	200	
					4,800

It may be seen that a single net figure for bad debts is debited to the profit and loss account, whilst the balance sheet is not affected at all.

Provisions for cash discounts

The principles involved in ascertaining the provision for cash discount allowed to customers is the same as for the provision for doubtful debts. Hence, having determined the figure to be provided for cash discount allowable, double entry may be effected by crediting the provision for discount allowed account and debiting the profit and loss account.* Having established the initial provision

* The balance sheet extract will show debtors less provision for accounts.

all that is required in subsequent periods is that the provision be adjusted, i.e. increased or decreased, according to the value of debtors and the percentage cash discount allowed.

The principles for ascertaining a provision for cash discounts receivable are again the same as for providing for doubtful debts, only the entries are reversed. Thus the provision for cash discounts receivable account is debited and the profit and loss account credited. The balance sheet will indicate creditors less provision for discount received.

Note: It is important to remember that when providing for cash discounts allowed the figure is calculated on the net value of debtors after deducting provision for doubtful debts. This is surely reasonable, as debtors who default cannot be allowed a discount.

Questions and problems

8–1 A business which commences business on January 1st 1985 receives a rate demand for £1,200 from the local authority in respect of the period January to March (inclusive) 1985. The bill is paid on January 20th.
On 8th April, a further demand for £2,600 covering April to September (inclusive) is received and paid on 16th April.
On 5th October a demand for another £2,600 is received to cover the period October 1985 to March 1986 (inclusive). This is paid on 17th October.
You are required:
(a) to write up the rates account as it would appear in the books of the business at 31st December 1985, indicating the amount transferred to the profit and loss account.
(b) To state how the balance of the rates account is dealt with in the final accounts for 1985.

Describe the accounting procedure to be followed when, in January, a £150 deposit on an advance hotel booking is received for a holiday to be taken in the following June.
Your answer should cover the period from the receipt of the deposit until the date of guest's departure.

(HCIMA)

8–2 From the following information prepare the laundry account in the nominal ledger of the Meedway Hotel Co. for the month of May.

(a) An accrued charge of £540 had been brought down from April.

(b) The following invoices were received from the Swanwhite Laundry Co.:

	£
4th May	1,600
11th May	750
18th May	1,200
25th May	640

(c) At the end of the month further charges of £300 had accrued for which no invoice had been received from the Swanwhite Laundry Co.

(d) Charges to guests' accounts during the month of May amounted to £2,550.

8–3 An hotel decided to keep a provision for bad debts of 5% of the debtors' figure outstanding at 31st December each year. From the following information you are required to write up the provision for bad debts account for the years 1985 and 1986 showing the amounts to be charged to profit and loss account. (If preferred, a separate bad debts account can be used.)

	£
Debtors at 31st December 1984	3,000
Debtors at 31st December 1985	3,800
Actual bad debts in 1985	160
Debtors at 31st December 1986	3,400
Actual bad debts in 1986	170

8–4 You are required, using the information given below, to prepare:

(a) the trading and profit and loss account for the Santor Post House for the year ended 31st March 1985; and

(b) the balance sheet as at that date.

The trial balance of the Santor Post House at 31st March 1985 was as follows:

	£	£
Capital		67,900
Freehold land and building	100,000	
Kitchen plant	9,000	
Stocks in hand (31st March 1984)	2,000	
Debtors and creditors	1,500	390
Provisions for doubtful debts		10
Cash at bank and in hand	800	
Loan interest	500	
Sales		150,000
Administration and other expenses	17,000	
Sales promotion expenses	1,200	
Wages and salaries	40,000	
Staff meals	1,000	
Purchases	55,300	
Loan		10,000
	£228,300	£228,300

You are given the following information:

1. The stocks in hand on 31st March 1985 were valued at £2,300;
2. Prepayments and accruals at 31st March 1985 were;

	Prepayments £	Accruals £
Administration expenses	1,600	700
Sales promotion expenses	100	250
Loan interest	–	500

8–5 The trial balance of the Blue Sky Hotel at 31st December 1986, was as follows:

	£	£
Capital		57,200
Stocks (1st January 1986)	1,500	
Loan from Q.		10,000
Leasehold premises	65,000	
Plant and equipment	8,000	
Debtors	600	
Creditors		500
Advertising and insurance	1,270	
Salaries and wages	11,000	
Rent and rates	900	
Discount received		70
Discount allowed	200	
Purchases	25,000	
Other income		1,200
Furniture	7,000	
Bank balance	1,000	
Drawings	2,400	
Heat and light	550	
Sundry expenses	450	
Cash in hand	100	
Sales		56,000
	£124,970	£124,970

The following should be taken into account:

(a) Rent outstanding amounted to £100.
(b) Insurance paid in advance £20.
(c) The proprietor estimated he had taken £80 worth of food during the year for his personal use. This had not been recorded.
(d) Advertising owing was £15.
(e) It was decided to set up a provision for doubtful debt equivalent to 5% of debtors.
(f) An invoice for plant repairs £25 had not been recorded in the books.
(g) Stocks at 31st December were valued at £2,000.
(h) The loan from Q. was made on 30th June 1986, at an agreed interest of 8% per annum. This had not been paid.

You are required to:

(a) prepare a trading, profit and loss account for the year ended 31st December 1986; and
(b) a balance sheet as at that date.

Chapter Nine

Depreciation, Replacement and Disposal of Fixed Assets

All expenditure incurred in purchasing assets which are to be utilized over more than one trading period is termed capital expenditure (referred to in Chapter 2) or said to be 'capitalized'. When purchasing such assets the total to be capitalized, i.e. debited to an asset account, will include the price, carriage and insurance thereon, installation costs and other costs incurred in preparing the asset for initial use.

Depreciation of fixed assets

As these assets are to be bought and maintained to generate profit over several trading periods then it follows that a charge should be made to each period benefiting from them. This charge, known as depreciation, is not merely a system of sharing out the cost of the asset over its useful life, but a method by which normal wear and tear, passage of time and possible obsolescence may be provided for.

Depreciation may be recorded by crediting each asset account and debiting a depreciation account with individual annual depreciation charges to be written off each year. This completed, the depreciation account balance may then be transferred to the profit and loss account. A more modern alternative which has gained much favour is to credit an individual provision for depreciation account for each group of assets, and debit the profit and loss account. This results in the asset remaining at cost in the ledger and provides an annual accumulation of depreciation in the provision account. This further enables the assets to be listed in the balance sheet at cost less the aggregate depreciation to date. It is the alternative treatment which has mainly been adopted in the following text although both treatments are found in practice. Again, the reader is reminded that prior to ledger postings transactions should be passed through the general journal, and this applies fully to depreciation.

There are several methods of calculating depreciation, of which the four most relevant to the hotel and catering industry are examined below.

Method 1 – straight line method

To implement this method (see Exhibit 9–1) known also as the fixed instalment method, three factors must be available and a simple formula applied:

(a) The initial cost of the asset.
(b) The estimated useful life of the asset.
(c) The expected residual or disposal value of the asset.

$$\frac{\text{Initial cost} - \text{Expected disposal value}}{\text{Estimated useful life in years}}$$

Exhibit 9–1

On 1st January 1984 a business purchased an item of machinery costing £1,000. The machine's estimated useful life is three years, with an expected disposal value of £100.

The formula may be applied as follows:

$$\frac{£1,000 - £100}{3 \text{ years}}$$

giving an annual charge against profit of £300 per year and leaving a disposal value of £100.

Machinery Account

1984	£	
Jan. 1 Bank	1,000	

Provision for Depreciation of Machinery Account

	£		£
1984		1984	
Dec. 31 Balance c/d	300	Dec. 31 Profit & loss a/c	300
	300		300
1985		1985	
Dec. 31 Balance c/d	600	Jan. 1 Balance b/d	300
		Dec. 31 Profit & loss a/c	300
	600		600
1986		1986	
Dec. 31 Balance c/d	900	Jan. 1 Balance b/d	600
		Dec. 31 Profit & loss a/c	300
	900		900
		1987	
		Jan. 1 Balance b/d	900

Profit and Loss Account (extract) for year ended 31st Dec. 1984		Balance Sheet (extract) as at 31st Dec. 1984		
	£		£	£
Depreciation:		*Fixed assets*		
Machinery 300		Machinery at cost	1,000	
		Less:		
		Aggregate depreciation	300	
				700

Profit and Loss Account (extract) for year ended 31st Dec. 1985		Balance Sheet (extract) as at 31st Dec. 1985		
	£		£	£
Depreciation:		*Fixed assets*		
Machinery 300		Machinery at cost	1,000	
		Less:		
		Aggregate depreciation	600	
				400

It may be seen in Exhibit 9–1 above that in the first year (ended 31st December 1984) the profit and loss account is debited with the £300 annual depreciation charge and the provision for depreciation of machinery account is credited £300. The balance sheet at that date shows the machinery at cost, i.e. £1,000 less aggregate depreciation to date of £300, indicating the true book

127

value of the machinery of £700 at that date.* In the second year (ended 31st December 1985) the profit and loss account charge is again £300 and the reader will notice that the provision account has increased from £300 to £600 by virtue of the current depreciation charge. Hence, in the balance sheet the depreciation to date shows an aggregate of £600 leaving the net book value of the machinery at £400. In the subsequent year the recording procedure is repeated.

Method 2 – reducing balance method

This method (see Exhibit 9–2), known also as the diminishing balance method, is adopted by writing off a fixed percentage of depreciation on the reducing value in the asset account. The percentage required under this method must usually be from two to three times that used by the straight line method.

Exhibit 9–2

Using the same figures as for the straight line method the result of the reducing balance method after three years' depreciation may be seen below:

	£
Original machinery cost (1st Jan. 1984)	1,000
Less: $\frac{33\frac{1}{3}}{100}$ × £1,000 depreciation (31st Dec. 1984)	333 (approx)
Net book value	667 – reducing balance
Less: $\frac{33\frac{1}{3}}{100}$ × £667 depreciation (31st Dec. 1985)	222 (approx.)
Net book value	445 – reducing balance
Less: $\frac{33\frac{1}{3}}{100}$ × £445 depreciation (31st Dec. 1985)	148 (approx.)
Net book value	297 – reduced balance

It will be observed that at the end of the third year, using the straight line method, all but £100 (the disposal value) had been written off, whereas here with the reducing balance method, Exhibit 9–2 above, there is still £197 (£297 − £100) depreciation yet to be written off. If then the percentage is increased to 55%, i.e. approximately doubled, the result would be as follows:

---

* If the balance sheet were prepared in vertical form then the layout of the asset and its aggregate depreciation would appear in the style of Exhibit 13–7 in Chapter 13.

	£
Original machinery cost (1st Jan. 1984)	1,000

Less: $\dfrac{55}{100}$ × £1,000 depreciation (31st Dec. 1984)   550

Net book value   450 – reducing balance

Less: $\dfrac{55}{100}$ × £450 depreciation (31st Dec. 1985)   247 (approx.)

Net book value   203 – reducing balance

Less: $\dfrac{55}{100}$ × £203 depreciation (31st Dec. 1986)   112 (approx.)

Approximate disposal value   91 – reduced balance

Although the final balance figure of £91 is not exactly the disposal value of £100, for all practical purposes it is satisfactory. If a more exact result is required then the percentage should be fractionally decreased below 55%.

Note: The ledger accounts and profit and loss account and balance sheet extracts have been omitted as it is the figures which differ from Exhibit 9–1 and not the double entry recordings.

Method 3 – revaluation method

This is a method employed to arrive at the annual depreciation of assets which it is not possible, in normal circumstances, to treat by usual depreciation methods, e.g. cutlery, crockery, glassware, loose kitchen equipment, investment, etc. In Exhibit 9–3 below the calculation and recording is demonstrated.

Exhibit 9–3

The depreciation charge is determined in the following manner:

	£
Opening stocks of china, etc. (1st Jan. 1986)	1,700
Add: Purchases of china and glass during the year	800
	2,500
Less: Closing stocks of china, etc. (31st Dec. 1986)	1,850
Value consumed (depreciation charge)	650

The accounts and extracts will appear as follows:

129

China, Glass and Cutlery Account

1986		£	1986		£
Jan. 1	Balance b/d	1,700	Dec. 31	Profit & loss a/c	650
	Bank	800		Balance c/d	1,850
		2,500			2,500
1987					
Jan. 1	Balance b/d	1,850			

Profit and Loss Account (extract) for year ended 31st Dec. 1986		Balance Sheet (extract) as at 31st Dec. 1986		
	£		£	£
Depreciation:		*Fixed assets*		
China, etc.	650	China, etc.	2,500	
		Less:		
		Depreciation	650	
				1,850

It will be noticed that as there is no accumulation of depreciation building up during the life of the china, etc., there is no need for a provision for depreciation account. Hence depreciation may be credited in the asset account.

Method 4 – replacement method

This method allows the initial capital outlay and additions to assets to remain in the books at cost and charge replacements to revenue, i.e. against profit. It has the important practical ingredient of simplicity although, in periods of extensive replacements, the smaller firms' profits may be severely affected. Grand Metropolitan Hotels Limited, for instance, in their annual report (30th September 1984), state they charge replacements of furniture and equipment in their hotels and catering premises to revenue.

Replacement of fixed assets

The four methods of providing for depreciation charges explained above are important techniques of accounting, but alone they lack a vital practical factor – cash. When an asset has been depreciated (written down) to a residual, disposal or nil value it is fair to assume that it will need replacing with a similar asset. Therefore, if cash has not been allocated or saved (even to the extent of an initial deposit) then it is likely that additional expense may be incurred in borrowing cash from outside sources to finance a replacement.

However, the sinking fund principle takes into account both the book entry aspect of actually depreciating an asset and also provides for eventual replacement.

The sinking fund principle is operated as follows:

At the end of each year a specific figure is set aside out of profit, whilst at the same time a predetermined cash sum is invested in gilt-edged securities,* e.g. government stocks, of which the invested sum should be equal to the profit set aside. When the asset has reached the end of its life the investments are realized, thus providing cash to purchase another.

Pertinent examples of the need for lump sums of cash by specific dates are the redemption of a liability, e.g. a loan, or the premium payable for the lease of land.

Exhibit 9–4 demonstrates the accounting treatment.

Exhibit 9–4

On 1st January 1984 the Z. Hotel purchased the lease of some land for £60,000, the lease having three years to run before being renewed.

Leasehold Land Account

1984		£	1986		£
Jan. 1 Bank		60,000	Dec. 31 Sinking fund a/c		60,000
1986				Balance c/d	60,000
Dec. 31 Bank		60,000			
		120,000			120,000
1987					
Jan. 1 Balance b/d		60,000			

* Investment interest received is credited in the sinking fund account and the cash reinvested requiring a debit entry in the sinking fund investment account. In Exhibit 9–4 interest has been omitted for the sake of simplicity.

Sinking Fund Account

1984		£	1984		£
Dec. 31 Balance c/d		20,000	Dec. 31 Profit & Loss a/c		20,000
		20,000			20,000
1985			1985		
Dec. 31 Balance c/d		40,000	Jan. 1 Balance b/d		20,000
			Dec. 31 Profit & loss a/c		20,000
		40,000			40,000
1986			1986		
Dec. 31 Leasehold land a/c		60,000	Jan. 1 Balance b/d		40,000
			Dec. 31 Profit & loss a/c		20,000
		60,000			60,000

Sinking Fund Investment Account

1984		£	1984		£
Dec. 31 Bank		20,000	Dec. 31 Balance c/d		20,000
1985			1985		
Jan. 1 Balance b/d		20,000	Dec. 31 Balance c/d		40,000
Dec. 31 Bank		20,000			
		40,000			40,000
1986			1986		
Jan. 1 Balance b/d		40,000	Dec. 31 Bank		40,000

In Exhibit 9–4 above the setting aside of profits and the investment of an equal amount of cash are completed simultaneously. The double entry being effected by debiting the profit and loss account and crediting the sinking fund account, i.e. setting aside profits, and crediting the cash book and debiting the sinking fund investment with cash equivalent to the profits set aside. The procedure is continued until the end of the third year. The final amount of profit is set aside and the sinking fund account is closed, and the balance transferred to the leasehold land account eliminating the asset balance therein. The equal amount of cash normally invested is retained, the reason being that as the end of the final year has been reached the cash which would normally be invested, together with the realized investments, is required to finance the premium renewal on the expired lease.

It is hoped that the sinking fund application brings home the necessity for management at all levels to be aware that *profit* is not an alternative term for *cash*. Consequently, depreciating or setting aside profit alone need not render available a single penny in terms of hard cash. Therefore, if this method of providing for asset replacement is not desired, management must include such foreseeable capital expenditure in their cash budgeting programme (explained fully in Chapter 6, Vol. 2).

Depreciation of additions to fixed assets

Where certain additions are made to an existing group of assets, e.g. machinery, motor vehicles, office equipment, etc., then depreciation must be considered. Below are enumerated three alternative suggestions as to how this may be based:

(a) By writing depreciation off the balance of the asset at the commencement of an accounting period, thus ignoring the additions in that period.
(b) Writing depreciation off the balance of the asset at the end of an accounting period, thus including additions for a full year's charge regardless of when they were purchased.
(c) By depreciating on a proportional time basis, so an asset purchased on 1st August would, at the end of the year, be depreciated by five-twelfths – and so on.

It will be apparent that, although the first two alternatives are not completely accurate, for practical purposes they have the advantage of simplicity.

Disposal of fixed assets

Normally, when an asset has reached the end of its useful life it is sold either by way of part-exchange on a new asset, or for scrap value. The entries made in the ledger will depend on the method used in recording depreciation. Where depreciation is credited to the asset account then the cash received on disposal is credited therein, the balancing figure representing a profit or loss on sale which is recorded in the profit and loss account at the end of the period. On the other hand, in the case where a separate provision for depreciation account is maintained then it is advisable to open a separate account named disposal, or sale, of assets.

Using the information in Exhibit 9–1 and assuming the machinery was sold on 4th January 1987 for £150, then the recording will be as follows:

Exhibit 9–5

Machinery Account

1987		£	1987		£
Jan. 1	Balance b/d	1,000	Jan. 4	Asset disposal a/c	1,000

Provision for Depreciation on Machinery Account

1987		£	1987		£
Jan. 4	Asset disposal a/c	900	Jan. 1	Balance b/d	900

Assets Disposal Account

1987		£	1987		£
Jan. 4	Machinery	1,000	Jan. 4	Depreciation	900
	Profit on sale	50		Cash	150
		1,050			1,050

Profit and Loss Account (extract) for year ended 31st Dec. 1987		Balance Sheet (extract) as at 31st Dec. 1987
Profit on sale of machinery	£ 50	Nil

In Exhibit 9–5 above the asset at cost and depreciation balances are transferred, by double entry, into the asset disposal account, the cash received on sale being credited therein and debited in the cash book. The difference on the disposal account represents a profit or loss, in this case a profit of £50, which is entered in the profit and loss account when final accounts are prepared. The closing of the machinery and depreciation provision accounts naturally results in the withdrawal of them from the next balance sheet, at the end of the year (indicated as blank).

Questions and problems

9–1 You are required to state:
   (a) what you understand by 'depreciation';
   (b) the reasons for making a provision for depreciation in balance sheets and profit and loss accounts; and
   (c) three accounting methods of providing for depreciation, with a description of each. What are the advantages and disadvantages of each method?

9–2 (a) Record the following items in a kitchen equipment account, calculating depreciation at 10% per annum on a straight line basis. (Items purchased before 30th June are depreciated fully in that year, and items after that date are not depreciated in that financial year.)

		£
1st Jan. 1985	Purchased equipment	4,000
31st Mar. 1985	Purchased equipment	8,000
30th Sept. 1986	Purchased equipment	6,000
2nd Jan. 1987	Sold equipment purchased on 1st January 1985 for	3,000

The account should be balanced at the end of each of the years 1985, 1986 and 1987 (show working).

(b) 'Since we now have a maintenance department and all equipment is on scheduled maintenance we no longer need to charge depreciation in the accounts.'
Comment on this statement.

9–3 Below is a company's summarized draft balance sheet at 30th April 1986:

Assets	£
Plant and equipment	40,000
Sinking fund investments	35,000
Cash at bank	80,000
	£155,000

Represented by:	£
Share capital	100,000
Sinking fund	35,000
Profit and loss account balance	20,000
	£155,000

The old plant and equipment has reached the end of its useful life and is sold for scrap for £2,500. It is replaced by new plant and equipment costing £50,000. The sinking fund investments are realized and the additional amount required for the purchase of the new plant and equipment is paid out of the bank balance.

You are required to draft out the company's balance sheet after the above transactions have taken place.

9–4 T. Herd is a sole trader operating the Waterside Restaurant. The trial balance overleaf was extracted from the books of the business on 31st December 1986.

You are required to prepare a trading and profit and loss account for the year ended 31st December 1986 and a balance sheet as at that date after taking into account the following:

(a) Stock at 31st December 1986 was valued at £3,000.

(b) £700 of the rates paid is in respect of the first quarter of 1987.

(c) An electricity bill of £600 in respect of the last quarter of 1986 has not yet been entered in the books.

(d) Make a provision for bad debts of £200.

(e) Depreciate furniture and equipment by 10% per annum. Cutlery, linen and china was revalued at £5,400 on 31st December 1986.

	Dr £	Cr £
Capital of T. Herd at 1st January 1986		120,000
Purchases and sales	121,000	280,000
Purchases returns		5,000
Wages and salaries	92,000	
National insurance	7,000	
Discounts received		2,200
Debtors and creditors	3,000	7,000
Bank balance	12,900	
Cash in hand	1,400	
Drawings by T. Herd	22,000	
Premises	93,000	
Furniture and equipment	27,000	
Cutlery, linen and china	5,700	
Laundry	4,000	
Gas and electricity	4,000	
Rates	3,000	
Insurance	1,500	
Telephone and postage	1,700	
Repairs and maintenance	8,000	
Advertising	3,000	
Stock at 1st January 1986	4,000	
	414,200	414,200

9–5 On 31 March 1986 the following balances appeared in the books of C. Mack, caterer.

	Dr £	Cr £
Capital		12,000
Drawings	1,100	
Bank current account	3,233	
Bank deposit account	508	
Bank deposit interest		8
Cash	54	
Stationery	181	
Staff meals	1,120	
Debtors & creditors	1,500	947
Discounts		270
Furniture, fixtures and fittings	1,600	
General expenses	1,110	
Leasehold premises (cost £10,000)	8,000	
Purchase & sales	10,140	20,743
Returns	232	
Salaries & wages	2,790	
Stock, 1 October 1985	2,400	
	33,968	33,968

Prepare a trading and profit and loss account for the half-year ended 31st March 1986 and a balance sheet as at that date, taking into consideration the following:

(a) Value of stock 31 March 1986 £2,510.
(b) Leasehold premises are to be written down at the rate of 10% per annum on the original cost.
(c) Bank deposit interest accrued, not yet entered in the books £12.
(d) Of the general expenses (£1,110), £65 is in respect of insurance in advance for the next half-year.
(e) £93 for salaries and wages have not yet been paid.

(HCIMA)

137

Chapter Ten
Incomplete Records

Although the ideal method of maintaining comprehensive accounting records appears, at first sight, to be on the double-entry principle, i.e. recording the twofold aspect of each business transaction, in practice many of the smaller and medium-sized establishments do not adopt this system. The reasons often expressed for not operating a 'complete' recording system are those of cost, lack of understanding of the relevance of accurate and detailed records and, particularly in the smaller businesses, the absence of the need for over-sophistication of accounting information.

Capital or revenue approach

A system which does not facilitate the recording of double entry is aptly termed 'single entry' or 'incomplete records'. In this field two distinct forms of situation are apparent:
   (a) where, because of the absence of sufficient information, the trading results cannot be ascertained by the more usual method of constructing a trading, profit and loss account (capital approach), and
   (b) where all the information is available or can be determined from existing information allowing a trading, profit and loss account to be constructed in the normal manner (revenue approach).
As stated, in the first situation a revenue (profit and loss) approach cannot be made but a capital (balance sheet) approach is possible. On reflection of previous sole-trader balance sheets it will be remembered that the capital at the end of a trading period is calculated thus:

	£
Capital at the beginning of the period	xxx
Add/Less: Profit/Loss	xx
	xxx
Add: Additional capital introduced (cash/other assets)	xx
	xxx
Less: Personal drawings (cash, goods, services, etc.)	xx
Capital at the end of the period	xxx

Opening and closing capital balances may also be determined by calculating the assets minus liabilities at the beginning and end of each period. Clearly, if five figures are connected together and any four are known then the fifth may be determined. The same principle applies regardless of the number of figures.

In the second situation the revenue approach is made by means of constructing summaries in ledger account form and identifying and including missing figures within the summaries and subsequently preparing final accounts.

To understand both approaches clearly it is thought best to consider an example (see Exhibit 10–1) containing sufficient information to allow the implementation of both capital and revenue approaches.

Exhibit 10–1

Q. commenced business on 1st January 1986 his trading period concluding on 31st December annually. On 30th September 1986 his financial position was as follows:

Statement of Affairs at 30th September 1986

	£	£		£	£
Capital		29,000	*Fixed assets*		
			Premises at cost		24,000
			Furniture, etc., at		
			cost		4,000
Current liabilities			*Current assets*		
Creditors	700		Stocks	1,000	
Accrued expenses	300		Debtors	600	
	——	1,000	Bank	400	
				——	2,000
		30,000			30,000

The following information is available:

1. Q's initial capital was £23,000 and his drawings were:

	Jan.–Sept.	£3,700
	Oct.–Dec.	£600

2. Sales were:

	Jan.–Sept.	£60,000
	Oct.–Dec.	£12,000

3. Purchases: Oct.–Dec.   £12,000

4. Expenses paid during Oct.–Dec. were £4,500, of which £200 related to the following year. There were no unpaid expenses at the end of the year.

5. All purchases and sales were on credit and the gross profit margin was a constant 40% on sales.

6. Closing stocks were valued at cost.

7. During Oct.–Dec. £11,500 was paid to creditors and £11,700 received from debtors. The latter debtors all arose during the period Jan.–Sept.

8. Provide a bad-debts provision at the end of the year equal to 1% of debtors.

9. A premises extension costing £3,000 was completed during Oct.–Dec.

10. Depreciation of 2% has been decided on furniture, etc., for the year ended 31st December, and is to be allocated on a time basis.

Prepare a trading, profit and loss accounts for year ended 31st December 1986 and a balance sheet at that date.

For the period January to September method (b) cannot be used, as without details of cash payments made neither purchases nor expenses can be independently ascertained, therefore the alternative method (a), the capital approach, is demonstrated. The first step is to calculate a profit figure.

	£	
Capital at 30th September 1986	29,000	(per statement of affairs)
Less: Capital at 1st January 1986	23,000	(1)
	6,000	
Add: Drawings	3,700	(1)
Profit per method (a)	9,700	
Less: Depreciation of furniture, etc. (¾ × £80)	60	(10)
NET PROFIT	9,640	

Q.'s Trading, Profit and Loss Account
for period 1st January to 30th September 1986

	£		£
Purchases (balancing item)	37,000	Sales (2)	60,000
Less: Stocks (30th Sept. 1986)			
(per statement of affairs)	1,000		
COST OF GOODS SOLD	36,000		
GROSS PROFIT (40% of £60,000)	24,000		
	60,000		60,000
Depreciation:		GROSS PROFIT	24,000
Furniture, etc. (¾ of £80)	60		
Expenses (balancing item)	14,300		
NET PROFIT (per calculation)	9,640		
	24,000		24,000

The difference between a balance sheet and statement of affairs is basically that the former gives more information than the latter, e.g. opening capital, profit or loss attained, proprietor's drawings, etc. 'Balancing item' refers to a figure not available from the records but deduced by virtue of it being the missing figure. The balancing items 'purchases' and 'expenses' in the above revenue account are obtained by plotting in the information supplied and determining the missing figures as being the difference in each case. It is important to understand that in the above trading, profit and loss account the net profit was ascertained first.

For the period October to December method (b) may be used. The first step is to open up the summary accounts. These are similar to control accounts, for instance a debtors' summary account is constructed with the same information and in the same way as a sales ledger control account, which itself is a summary of the total transactions posted in the sales ledger.

Bank Summary

1986		£	1986		£
Oct. 1	Balance (per state-		Oct./Dec.	Creditors (7)	11,500
	ment of affairs)	400		Expenses (4)	4,500
	Debtors (7)	11,700		Drawings (1)	600
Dec. 31	Balance c/d	7,500		Premises	
				extension (9)	3,000
		19,600			19,600
				Balance b/d	7,500

Debtors' Summary

1986		£	1986		£
Oct. 1	Balance (per statement of affairs)	600	Oct./Dec.	Bank (7)	11,700
	Sales (1)	12,000	Dec. 31	Balance c/d	900
		12,600			12,600
	Balance b/d	900			

Creditors' Summary

1986		£	1986		£
Oct./Dec.	Bank (7)	11,500	Oct. 1	Balance (per statement of affairs)	700
Dec. 31	Balance c/d	1,200		Purchases (3)	12,000
		12,700			12,700
				Balance b/d	1,200

Expenses Summary

1986		£	1986		£
Oct./Dec.	Bank (4)	4,500	Oct. 1	Balance – owing (per statement of affairs)	300
				Profit & loss a/c	4,000
				Balance – prepaid (4)	200
		4,500			4,500
	Balance b/d	200			

It will be observed from the above that by preparing the summary accounts by double entry (except the simple summaries, e.g. premises) the information is pieced together so enabling final accounts to be constructed in the normal manner set out below:

Q.'s Trading, Profit and Loss Account
for period 1st October to 31st December 1986

	£		£
Stocks (1st Oct. 1986)	1,000	Sales (2)	12,000
Add: Purchases (3)	12,000		
	13,000		
Less: Stocks (31st Dec. 1986)			
(balancing item)	5,800		
COST OF GOODS SOLD	7,200		
GROSS PROFIT (40% of £12,000)	4,800		
	12,000		12,000
Expenses	4,000	GROSS PROFIT	4,800
Provision for bad debts (8)	9		
Depreciation:			
Furniture, etc. (10)	20		
NET PROFIT	771		
	4,800		4,800

It may be seen in the above trading, profit and loss account that the only missing figure was closing stocks, which again is deduced as being the balancing item.

Q.'s Balance Sheet as at 31st December, 1986

	£	£	£		£	£	£
Capital				*Fixed Assets*	Cost	Depr'n	Net
1st Jan. 1986		23,000		Premises	27,000	–	27,000
Add: Net profit				Furniture etc.	4,000	80	3,920
Jan./Sept.	9,640				31,000	80	30,920
Oct./Dec.	771						
		10,411					
		33,411					
Less: Drawings							
Jan./Sept.	3,700						
Oct./Dec.	600						
		4,300					
			29,111	*Current Assets*			
Current Liabilities				Stocks		5,800	
Creditors		1,200		Debtors	900		
Bank overdraft		7,500		*Less:* Provn. bad			
			8,700	debts	9		
						891	
				Prepaid expenses		200	
							6,891
			37,811				37,811

In preparation of the above balance sheet it will be seen that the true movement of capital is reliant on the inclusion of net profit and drawings determined from each period.

Questions and problems

10-1 R. Cromwell owns a small restaurant but does not keep records on a double entry system. The following information is available.

Balance Sheets

	1st Jan. 1986 £	31st Dec. 1986 £		1st Jan. 1986 £	31st Dec. 1986 £
Capital	49,650	53,800	Freehold premises	37,000	37,000
Trade creditors	2,420	3,800	Furniture and		
Wages owing	–	450	equipment	15,250	13,600
Bank overdraft	4,000	–	Van	2,200	1,900
			Trade debtors	1,200	2,300
			Cash at bank	–	2,670
			Petty cash in hand	420	580
	56,070	58,050		56,070	58,050

During the year Cromwell's personal drawings amounted to £15,400. The reduction in the value of furniture and equipment and the van is due to depreciation. He had written off £260 of debts as bad and his trade expenses (in addition to wages owing) amounted to £12,950.

You are required to draw up a statement showing Cromwell's net profit/loss and gross profit/loss for the year.

10-2 From the following information you are required to prepare C. Lagg's trading and profit and loss account for the year ended 31st December and a balance sheet at that date.

C. Lagg's assets and liabilities were:
1st January, – Creditors £14,200; Rent owing £500; Stock £27,000; Debtors £23,000; Fixtures and fittings £15,000; Goodwill £20,000; Cash at bank £5,000.
31st December, – Creditors £15,050; Rent owing £250; Stock £26,500; Debtors £27,850; Rates in advance £150; Fixtures and fittings £15,000; Goodwill £20,000.
Receipts during year – Cash sales £25,000; Cash from debtors £113,000; Payment during year – to creditors £78,670; Rent and rates £1,700; Salaries and wages £21,790; General expenses £11,000; Drawings £7,500; Cash purchases £3,940.

The following have also to be taken into account.
(a) Fixtures and fittings to be depreciated by 5%.
(b) Provision for bad debts to be 5% of debtors (to nearest £) at both dates.
(c) Discounts allowed were £3,200 and discounts received were £2,400.
(d) Goods taken for own use were £1,290.

10–3 George Main requests that you prepare his trading and profit and loss account for the year ended 30th June 1986 and balance sheet at that date, from the following information.

Asset and liabilities were:
1st July 1985 – Fixtures and fittings £12,000; Stock £8,000; Debtors £1,000; Creditors £3,500; Light and heating owing £40; Rates in advance £100; Cash £2,630.
30th June 1986 – Fixtures and fittings £12,000; Stock £9,000; Debtors £1,600; Creditors £3,000; Rent owing £250; Wages owing £90; Rates in advance £120.
Receipts during year – from debtors £51,250.
Payments during year – to creditors £40,100; Carriage inwards £840; Wages £4,590; Sundry expenses £250; Printing, stationery and advertising £560; Drawings £3,040; Rent and rates £1,250; Heating and lighting £690.

You are also informed that:
(a) goods taken for own use amounted to £400;
(b) fixtures and fittings to be depreciated by 10%.

Chapter Eleven

Accounts of Non-Profit-Making Organizations

There are many organizations in existence which do not set out with the prime object of making a profit. These include such organizations as sports and social clubs, art societies, professional institutes and student associations. Nevertheless, whatever the pursuit of such bodies may be, it is usual that finance and financial transactions have to be accounted for and recorded in a proper manner for presentation to members at the organization's annual general meeting. However, this does not mean to suggest that a complete double-entry accounting system should be maintained; on the contrary, a large number of associations maintain, as it were, a system of incomplete records.

The main source of revenue of non-profit-making organizations is normally derived from members' subscriptions, other income generally tending to be in the form of donations and as a result of sporting and social occasions. Expenditure, on the other hand, is usually incurred in providing premises and facilities for their members' participation and enjoyment.

Records maintained by clubs and societies may vary from simple note books or diaries to modern, sophisticated computerized accounting systems, according to size, objects and requirements. The physical book-keeping is in many instances comparable with a commercial business of a proportionate size. The major difference between profit and non-profit-making organizations really amounts to different terminology for similar items. For instance, a commercial business records its normal revenue in a sales account whereas an association usually records its revenue in a subscriptions account, and so on.

Receipts and payments accounts

It is usual for clubs and societies to record receipts and payments of money in a cash book, ruled to the particular requirement. At the end of the society's financial year, the entries in the cash book are summarized and the summaries entered in a receipts and payments account. Some clubs consider this sufficient for presentation to its members, as it discloses the cash balance at the beginning of the year, total receipts and payments of cash during the year and the balance of cash in hand at the end of the year. For the recently formed association, a receipts and payments account may be sufficient but in the case of an association having assets, other than cash, and liabilities, then, as a statement indicating the financial state, it is completely inadequate. The reason for this is that such an account considers only part of a year's income and expenditure, which means it neither takes into account income due or appertaining to another year nor expenditure occurring or paid in advance and therefore, due to these failings, it will not disclose a profit (surplus) or loss (deficit).

Income and expenditure account

To achieve an adequate report on the financial state of a society, as in all undertakings, proper financial statements should be presented. For this purpose an income and expenditure account, compiled in the same manner as a profit and loss account, and a balance sheet are prepared. The resulting excess of income over expenditure, or excess of expenditure over income, as the case may be, is known usually as a surplus or deficit respectively. The reason for not normally meeting the terms profit or loss in use is that technically an association or society does not exist to make a profit and therefore cannot sustain a loss.

Balance sheet

The balance sheet of a non-profit-making organization is similar to that of a sole trader, with the exception that the term 'accumulated fund' replaces in most instances that of capital. Of course, for all intents and purposes they are both the same and may be calculated in a similar manner to each other, i.e. assets minus liabilities.

Ancillary revenue accounts

Some non-profit-making organizations may wish to ascertain if a surplus or deficit has occurred within a particular area of activity or service. For instance, a club may produce a magazine, run social occasions, or operate a bar or restaurant and, although it is not generally desired to profit from members, it is important to determine whether or not the event or activity is financially breaking even. To ascertain this a revenue account, in the form of a trading account, is prepared as shown in Exhibit 11–1. It is important to note that, if such a revenue account is prepared, then all income and expenditure appertaining to the event or service should be entered therein, i.e. in the case of a bar account, barman's wages and sundry bar expenses should be entered in the account and the balance, representing a surplus or deficit, transferred into the income and expenditure account.

Exhibit 11–1 is an example of the preparation of final accounts of a non-profit-making organization.

Exhibit 11–1

The treasurer of the Queen's County Sports Club prepared the following receipts and payments account for the year ended 30th June 1985 from *bank statements* received during the year:

Receipts	£	£	Payments	£	£
Cash at 1st July 1984:			Purchase of furniture		850
In hand	225		Wages: Groundsman	4,500	
As per bank statements:			Barman	1,700	
Current account	500				6,200
Deposit account	1,175		Printing & stationery		275
		1,900	Bar purchases		14,150
Subscriptions		7,100	Telephone & insurance		175
Bar takings		20,500	Clubhouse rent		3,000
Bank interest		50	Cash at bank 30th June		
Donations		125	1985:		
			Current account	1,525	
			Deposit account	3,500	
					5,025
		29,675			29,675

The following information was obtained:

	June 1984 £	June 1985 £
(a) Telephone calls in arrears	40	30
(b) Insurance paid in advance	35	45
(c) Subscriptions: In arrears	175	240
In advance	12	160
(d) Value of bar stocks	900	1,050
(e) Cheques issued for bar purchases but not presented	300	140

You also ascertain that:

- (i) Bar receipts on 30th June 1985, totalling £220, were not paid into the bank until 1st July 1985.

- (ii) Furniture is to be depreciated at 10% (regardless of date of purchase).

- (iii) Donation to local charity £25.

You are requested to:

- (a) Compute the balance of the accumulated fund of the club as on 30th June 1984; and

- (b) Prepare separate bar and subscription accounts; and

- (c) Prepare an income and expenditure account for year ended 30th June 1985 and balance sheet at that date.

The accumulated fund at 30th June 1984 may be calculated by extracting the assets and liabilities at that date:

Accumulated Fund Computation

	£	£
Cash on hand		225
Cash in current account	500	
Less: Unpresented cheques	300	
	——	200
Cash in deposit account		1,175
Insurance paid in advance		35
Subscriptions in arrears		175
Bar stocks		900
		2,710
Less:		
Telephone calls in arrears	40	
Subscriptions in advance	120	
	——	160
Accumulated fund 30th June 1984		2,550

The bar and subscriptions accounts may be presented in the following manner:

Bar Account for year ended 30th June 1985

	£	£
Bar receipts (£20,500 + £220)		20,720
Stocks (1st July 1984)	900	
Add: Purchases during year	13,990	
	14,890	
Less: Stocks (30th June 1985)	1,050	
COST OF GOODS SOLD	13,840	
Add: Barman's wages	1,700	
		15,540
Bar surplus transferred to income and expenditure account		5,180

The figure of purchases £13,990 in the above bar account is determined as follows:

	£
Cheques paid (as per bank statements)	14,150
Less: Unpresented cheques 30th June 1984	300
	13,850
Add: Unpresented cheque 30th June 1985	140
Bar purchases for year	13,990

Subscriptions Account

1984		£	1984		£
July 1 Balance b/d – arrears		175	July 1 Balance b/d – prepaid		120
1985			June/July 1985:		
June 30 Income & expenditure a/c		7,125	Bank		7,100
Balance c/d – prepaid		160	1985		
			June Balance c/d – arrears		240
		7,460			7,460
1985			1985		
July 1 Balance b/d		240	July 1 Balance b/d		160

It should be noted that in the subscriptions account above the item £7,100 would in practice not be in total but a list of members' individual subscriptions received.

The income and expenditure account and balance sheet may be presented as set out below:

Queen's County Sports Club
Income and Expenditure Account for year ended
30th June 1985

	£	£
INCOME		
Subscriptions	7,125	
Bar surplus	5,180	
Donations	125	
Bank interest	50	
	———	12,480
Less: EXPENDITURE		
Groundsman's wages	4,500	
Printing and stationery	275	
Telephone and insurance	155	
Clubhouse rent	3,000	
Donation to local charity	25	
Depreciation:		
Furniture	85	
	———	8,040
EXCESS OF INCOME OVER EXPENDITURE		4,440

Queen's County Sports Club
Balance Sheet as at 30th June 1985

	£	£	£
FIXED ASSETS			
Furniture at cost		850	
Less: Depreciation		85	
			765
CURRENT ASSETS			
Bar stocks		1,050	
Subscriptions in arrears		240	
Insurance prepaid		45	
Cash at bank			
Current account (£1,525 − £140 − £25)		1,360	
Deposit account		3,500	
Cash in hand		220	
		6,415	
Less: CURRENT LIABILITIES			
Subscriptions in advance	160		
Telephone calls in arrears	30		
		190	
			6,225
			6,990
REPRESENTED BY:			
Accumulated fund			
1st July 1984			2,550
Add: Excess of income over expenditure			4,440
			6,990

Questions and problems

11–1 The following data is obtained from the books of the Downtown Social Club for 1985:

RECEIPTS	£
Members' subscriptions	15,000
Entrance fees	3,500
Bar receipts	31,300

PAYMENTS	
Cost of 2 new table-tennis tables	1,000
Bar purchases (liquor)	19,900
Bar wages	6,000
Heating and lighting bill	1,300
Advertising charge	500
Postage and stationery	200
Caretaker's wages	7,000
Cash balance at 1st January 1985	1,810
Cash balance at 31st December 1985	15,710

You are required to prepare the club's bar trading account and income and expenditure account for 1985 with a balance sheet as at 31st December 1985 taking into account the following:

1. Entrance fees are regarded as receipts of capital.

2. The subscriptions include £1,000 in respect of 1986.

3. Bar stocks were valued as follows:
   at 1st January 1985   £4,240
   at 31st December 1985   £4,800

4. At 1st January 1985 the club premises were valued at £125,000 and the furniture and equipment at £31,000.

5. The club's capital fund at 1st January 1985 stood at £162,050.

6. Depreciate the furniture and equipment by 10% on the balance at 1st January 1985.

7. The profit, or loss, on the bar trading account is to be transferred to the income and expenditure account.

(HCIMA)

11–2 The receipts and payments account of the Wellcome Club for the year ended 31st December is given below.
You are required to prepare an income and expenditure account and a balance sheet as at 31st December for presentation

to the club members at the general meeting taking into consideration the following:

(a) A separate bar account should be shown and the net profit on the bar transferred to income and expenditure account.

(b) At 1st January the club furniture and equipment stood at £4,000; charge depreciation at 10% p.a. on this figure.

(c) At 1st January the value of the furnishing was £1,250; depreciate these by £250.

(d) At 1st January the accumulated capital fund stood at £12,500.

(e) At 1st January the renovations fund stood at £2,675.

(f) The club has investments of £5,000.

(g) The bar stocks were:

1st January	£3,750
31st December	£4,150

(h) At 31st December the following accounts were owing:

Rent	£375
Printing and stationery	£100
Repairs	£65
Fuel	£225

(i) At 31st December rates paid in advance were £175.

(j) Of the subscriptions £50 referred to next year and £85 was owing at the end of the year.

(k) One-half of the surplus for the year is to be added to the accumulated fund, and one-half added to the renovations fund.

Receipts and Payments Account

	£		£
Opening balance	1,175	Rent and rates	2,800
Bar takings	20,290	Printing and stationery	600
Outside catering receipts		Repairs	435
(credit bar a/c)	1,250	Fuel and lighting	1,300
Subscriptions	2,265	Equipment	1,000
Garden fête net receipts	650	Cleaning and sundries	325
Investment income	250	Barman's wages	3,750
Donations	500	Caretaker's wages	1,250
		Additional bar help	600
		Bar purchases	12,340
		Closing balance	1,980
	26,380		26,380

(HCIMA)

Chapter Twelve

Accounts of Partnerships

Partnerships are usually formed to unite financial and technical resources and more often than not to enable the introduction of specialization and sharing of management functions.

Legal aspects

Partnership Act 1890

Section 1 of the Act defines a partnership as 'the relation which subsists between persons carrying on a business in common with a view of profit'.

Section 9 provides that every partner in a firm is liable jointly with the other partners for all debts and obligations of the firm incurred while he is a partner, even to the extent of his personal assets.

Section 24 provides that the interests of partners in the partnership property and their rights and duties in relation to the partnership shall be determined, subject to any agreement expressed or implied between the partners by the following rules:

1. All partners are entitled to an equal share in the capital and profits of the business, and must contribute equally towards the losses whether of capital or otherwise sustained by the firm.
2. The firm must indemnify every partner in respect of payments made and personal liabilities incurred by him –
   (a) in the ordinary and proper conduct of the business of the firm; or
   (b) in or about anything necessarily done for the preservation of the business or property of the firm.
3. A partner making, for the purpose of the partnership, any actual payment or advance beyond the amount of capital which he has agreed to subscribe i.e. a loan, is entitled to interest at the rate of 5% per annum from the date of payment or advance.

4. A partner is not entitled, for ascertainment of profits, to interest on the capital subscribed by him.
5. Every partner may take part in the management of the partnership business.
6. No partner shall be entitled to remuneration for acting in the partnership business.
7. No person may be introduced as a partner without the consent of all existing partners.
8. Any difference arising as to ordinary matters connected with the partnership business may be decided by a majority of the partners, but no change may be made in the nature of the partnership business without the consent of all existing partners.
9. The partnership books are kept at the place of business of the partnership (or principal place if there is more than one), and every partner may, when he thinks fit, have access and inspect and copy any of them.

Section 28 states 'partners are bound to render true accounts and full information of all things affecting the partnership to any partner or his legal representatives'.

Limited Partnership Act 1907

Section 4 provides that a limited partnership must consist of one or more 'general' partners (see kinds of partners below), who shall be liable for all debts and obligations of the firm, and one or more persons to be called limited partners, who shall at the time of entering into such partnership contribute thereto a sum or sums as capital or property valued at a stated amount, and who shall not be liable for the debts or obligations of the firm beyond the amount so contributed. The act also provides that a limited partner shall not during the continuance of the partnership, either directly or indirectly, draw out or receive back any part of his contribution, and if he does so draw out or receive back any such part shall be liable for the debts and obligations of the firm up to the amount so drawn out or received back. The Act states that a body corporate may be a limited partner.

Section 6 provides that a limited partner shall not take part in the management of the partnership business, and shall not have power to bind the firm, but that a limited partner may by himself or his agent at any time inspect the books of the firm and examine the state and prospects of the partnership business, and may advise the partners thereon. The Act provides that if a limited partner takes part in the management of the partnership business he is liable for all debts and obligations of the firm incurred while he so takes part in the management as though he were a general partner. (Accounting treatments relevant to limited partnerships are not discussed in this text – all accounting applies to a partnership consisting of general partners.)

Partnership size

With the exception of certain professions, e.g. solicitors, accountants and stockbrokers, partnerships are restricted to twenty persons.

Kinds of partners

Basically the law recognizes two kinds of partners, 'general' partners and 'limited' partners. In practice, however, reference is frequently made to 'active' and 'sleeping' partners. If a partner actually takes part in the running of a partnership business then he is referred to as an active partner, whereas a partner who does not take an active part in the running of a firm is referred to as a sleeping partner, but both in the eyes of the law are classed as general partners.

Partnership agreement (or deed)

Although a partnership agreement may be expressed or implied, it is frequently more satisfactory to have an agreement drawn up professionally so that each prospective partner is aware of his partnership terms. A list of the more important considerations are enumerated below:

(a) The duties and responsibilities of each partner.
(b) The amount of capital initially to be introduced by each partner.
(c) Whether the partners' capital contributions are to remain fixed or not.
(d) The proportions in which profits and losses are to be shared.
(e) The salaries, if at all, to be paid to each partner.
(f) The rates of interests:
　　(i) allowed on each partner's capital;
　　(ii) charged on each partner's drawings;
　　(iii) allowed on a loan from a partner.
(g) The method of maintaining and auditing accounts.
(h) The admission of new partners and the retirement of existing partners.

Partners' accounts

The maintenance of accounting records for partnerships are similar to those of any business. The difference occurs in respect of partners' personal accounts. For each partner a separate set of personal accounts, i.e. capital, drawings, etc., is maintained so enabling details of profits, drawings, interest and so on, to be recorded in the partners' own accounts.

Partners' capital

There are two approaches to dealing with partners' capital:

(a) *Fixed capital method*, where with the exception of withdrawals or the introduction of extra capital sums, a partner's capital remains at a fixed amount. Any profits, interest or drawings receivable or payable by the partners are accounted for in what is termed a 'current' account (no connection with a bank current account).
(b) *Alternative capital method*, in which the partners' capital is not kept at a fixed amount. All profits, interest and drawings are collected in the partners' capital account, in the same manner as that of a sole trader.

Profit and loss appropriation account

At the end of each trading period final accounts are prepared in a similar manner as for a sole trader excepting that net profit is adjusted and shared before being transferred to the partners' capital or current accounts. The profit adjustments and apportionments, namely interests, and salaries (if any), are made in a further section of the everyday form of trading, profit and loss account called a profit and loss appropriation account.

Below in Exhibit 12–1 the fixed and alternative capital methods and profit and loss appropriation account are illustrated.

Exhibit 12–1

On 1st January 1986 Long and Short went into partnership sharing profits in the ratio 3 : 2. On 31st December 1986, after preparation of the trading, profit and loss account, the following balances remained in their books:

	£
Capital account – Long	90,000
Capital account – Short	50,000
Drawings – Long	9,000
Drawings – Short	6,000
Loan from Long	10,000
Stocks	20,000
Debtors	37,500
Creditors	16,000
Cash at bank	8,750
Net profit – 1986 (per profit and loss account)	24,000
Fixed assets	108,750

The following has still to be taken into account:
  (a) Long is entitled to 5% loan interest.
  (b) Short has taken goods worth £150 for his own personal use.
  (c) Interest on capital: Long £3,000
                               Short £2,250
  (d) Interest on drawings: Long   £750
                             Short   £500
  (e) Short is entitled to a salary of £1,500 before profits are shared.
  (f) During the year Short introduced certain fixed assets into the business valued at £4,500.

If the fixed capital method is adopted then in the ledger the partners' capital and current accounts will appear as follows:

Capital Account – Long

		1986	£
		Dec. 31 Balance b/d	90,000

Capital Account – Short

1986		£	1986		£
Dec. 31 Balance c/d		54,500	Jan. 1 Bank		50,000
			Dec. 31 Sundry fixed assets		4,500
		54,500			54,500
			Dec. 31 Balance b/d		54,500

159

Current Account — Long

1986		£	1986		£
Dec. 31	Drawings	9,000	Dec. 31	Interest on capital	3,000
	Interest on drawings	750		Loan interest	
	Balance c/d	4,640		(5% × £10,000)	500
				Share of profits	
				(⅗ × £18,150)	10,890
		14,390			14,390
			Dec. 31	Balance b/d	4,640

Current Account – Short

1986		£	1986		£
Dec. 31	Drawings	6,000	Dec. 31	Interest on capital	2,250
	Goods taken	150		Salary	1,500
	Interest on			Share of profits	
	drawings	500		(⅖ × £18,150)	7,260
	Balance c/d	4,360			
		11,010			11,010
			Dec. 31	Balance b/d	4,360

The profit and loss appropriation account is constructed in exactly the same manner even though the fixed capital method or alternative capital method is adopted. Here, to assist the reader in identifying the double entry, the appropriation account is illustrated in the traditional manner whereas in the alternative capital method the appropriation account is presented in the more modern, vertical form. (See appropriation account below.)

It will be observed that in respect of profit adjustments and apportionments all double entries are completed between the partners' current accounts and the appropriation account. The £150 worth of goods taken by Short represents purchases not available for sale and therefore will reduce the purchases figure in the trading account and thereby increase profit.

The partnership balance sheet, presented vertically, would be as illustrated below.

Messrs Long and Short, Partners
Profit and Loss Appropriation Account for year ended 31st December 1986

Interest on Capital:	£	£	NET PROFIT b/d from	£	£
Long	3,000		Profit & Loss a/c		
Short	2,250		(£24,000 + £150)		24,150
		5,250			
Loan interest – Long		500	*Interest on Drawings:*		
Salary – Short		1,500	Long	750	
Share of profits:			Short	500	
Long					1,250
(³⁄₅ × £18,150)	10,890				
Short					
(²⁄₅ × £18,150)	7,260				
		18,150			
		25,400			25,400

Messrs. Long and Short, Partners Balance Sheet as at 31st December 1986

	£	£	£
FIXED ASSETS (£108,750 + £4,500)			113,250
CURRENT ASSETS			
Stocks		20,000	
Debtors		37,500	
Cash at bank		8,750	
		66,250	
Less: CURRENT LIABILITIES			
Creditors		16,000	
WORKING CAPITAL			50,250
CAPITAL EMPLOYED			163,500
FINANCED BY:			
PARTNERS' CAPITAL			
Long	90,000		
Short	54,500		
		144,500	
PARTNERS' CURRENT ACCOUNTS			
Long	4,640		
Short	4,360		
		9,000	
			153,500
LOAN ACCOUNT – Long			10,000
			163,500

In the event of a partner's current account having a debit balance, sometimes being referred to as a fictitious asset, then the balance may either be shown as a deduction from the other partners' current totals or on its own, below the current assets. The former option is preferred in practice as it offers a more accurate result than the latter which itself appears to increase the capital employed figure.

In the case of adopting the alternative capital method then in the ledger the partners' capital accounts will appear as below:

Capital Account – Long

1986		£	1986		£
Dec. 31	Drawings	9,000	Jan. 1	Bank	90,000
	Interests on		Dec. 31	Interest on capital	3,000
	drawings	750		Loan interest	
	Balance c/d	94,640		(5% × £10,000)	500
				Share of profits	
				(3/5 × £18,150)	10,890
		104,390			104,390
			Dec. 31	Balance b/d	94,640

Capital Account – Short

1986		£	1986		£
Dec. 31	Drawings	6,000	Jan. 1	Bank	50,000
	Goods taken	150	Dec. 31	Sundry fixed assets	4,500
	Interest on drawings	500		Interest on capital	2,250
	Balance c/d	58,860		Salary	1,500
				Share of profits	
				(2/5 × £3,630)	7,260
		65,510			65,510
			Dec. 31	Balance b/d	58,860

Messrs Long and Short, Partners
Profit and Loss Appropriation Account
for year ended 31st December 1986

	£	£	£
NET PROFIT (£24,000 + £150)			
from profit and loss account			24,150
Add: INTEREST ON DRAWINGS:			
Long		750	
Short		500	
		———	1,250
			25,400
			cont.

		£	£	£
Less:				
INTEREST ON CAPITAL:				
	Long	3,000		
	Short	2,250		
			5,250	
Loan interest –	Long		500	
Salary –	Short		1,500	
SHARE OF PROFITS:				
	Long ⅗	10,890		
	Short ⅖	7,260		
			18,150	
				25,400

The net assets indicating capital employed in the partnership business balance sheet (fixed capital method) are exactly the same as for the alternative capital method. It is the capital presentation which differs, as illustrated below:

Messrs Long and Short, Partners
Balance Sheet (extract) as at 31st December 1986

	£	£
FINANCED BY:		
PARTNERS' CAPITAL		
Long	94,640	
Short	58,860	
		153,500
LOAN ACCOUNT – Long		10,000
		163,500

Questions and problems

12–1 What are the advantages and disadvantages of limited partnerships?

12–2 Martin and Robert are in partnership, sharing profits equally. The partnership agreement provides *inter alia* that interest at 5% per annum is to be allowed to the partners on their capital accounts. The partnership balance sheet as at 1st January 1987 was as under:

Capital accounts:	£	£
Martin	30,000	
Robert	15,000	
		45,000
Current accounts:		
Martin	9,000	
Robert	6,000	
		15,000
Sundry liabilities		9,000
		69,000
Sundry assets		69,000

The profit after charging all expenses except interest on capital for the year ended 31st December 1987 was £36,750. Drawings during the year were Martin £10,500 and Robert £9,300.

Sundry liabilities at 31st December 1987 amounted to £6,000. The asset figures are not given and will have to be calculated from the data to complete the balance sheet.

You are required to prepare:
- (a) the profit and loss appropriation account for the year ended 31st December 1987; and
- (b) a balance sheet as at that date.

Chapter Thirteen
Accounts of Limited Companies

In the eyes of the law a company is a separate legal entity. It may enter into contracts and be sued for breach of contract. A company enjoys the advantage of perpetual succession, which means the death or withdrawal of its proprietors (shareholders) does not give cause for the company to cease trading.

Types of companies

Companies may be formed by:
1. Royal Charter, e.g. East India Company.
2. Special Act of Parliament, e.g. Mersey Docks and Harbour Board.
3. Registration under the Companies Act 1985.

Kinds of registered companies

Unlimited companies

These are companies which do not afford their members (shareholders) limitation in respect of debts incurred in the cause of trading. This means that in the event of an unlimited company defaulting, the shareholders become liable to make good such debts which have arisen.

Companies limited by guarantee

Refers to companies whose members each guarantee to contribute a certain sum of money in the event of the company being wound up. Professional bodies are among the few kinds of companies of this nature, e.g. Hotel, Catering and Institutional Management Association, Chartered Institute of Management Accountants, and so on.

Limited companies

These are companies which are 'limited by shares', that is to say in respect of debts or other financial crises occurring, the liability of the shareholders is restricted (limited) to the amount of their investment (shares) in the company. This kind of company forms by far the largest number in industry and commerce today and therefore discussion and explanation is centred on the limited company.

Limited companies

Limited companies may be divided into 'private' and 'public'. A private limited company is basically one which by virtue of its articles is restricted in the right to transfer its shares from person to person; is limited (exclusive of employees or past employees) to fifty shareholders; and is legally bound not to invite the public to subscribe for any shares or debentures of the company. From the foregone facts it may clearly be said that a public company is one which is not, in the legal sense, a private company, that is, it may transfer shares and offer shares to the public and there is no upper limit on its number of shareholders. The minimum number of shareholders allowed, by law, to form a private company is two and in the case of a public company is seven.

Below is a chart illustrating the types and kinds of companies:

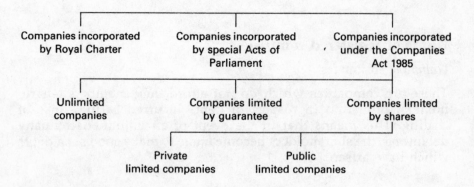

Incorporation of companies

In order to acquire incorporation both public and private companies must comply with the requirements of the Companies Act 1985. Among the requirements both public and private companies must submit to the Registrar of Companies certain documents, the two most important being the 'memorandum of association' and 'articles of association'.

Memorandum of association

The Act provides that the memorandum of association of every company must state, among other things:
  (a) The name of the company, with 'limited' as the last word of the name in the case of a company limited by shares or by guarantee.
  (b) The objects of the company.
  (c) The liability of shareholders.
  (d) The amount of its share capital and the division thereof into shares of a fixed amount.

Articles of association

The act provides that unlimited companies and companies limited by guarantee must submit articles of association wherefore a limited company may prepare its own articles of association but in the event of not doing so then a set of standard articles known as Table A will automatically apply to the company.

The articles of association are rules which govern the internal affairs of a company; such matters as the issue and forfeiture of shares, meeting procedure, directors' duties and responsibilities and shareholders' obligations and rights.

Preliminary or formation expenses

These are expenses incurred in forming a company and include such items as legal fees for drafting the memorandum and articles of association, registration fees, stamp duties and various printing costs. These expenses are debited in a preliminary expenses account.

Capital structure

The following list explains the terms used in connection with the capital of a limited company:

  (a) *Authorized or registered or nominal share capital.* All these terms similarly mean the maximum amount of share capital, stated in a company's memorandum of association, that the company has the power to issue.

(b) *Issued or subscribed share capital.* Both terms similarly mean the total nominal (face value) of shares allotted to members even though a certain number may be only partly paid.

(c) *Called-up share capital.* This refers to that part of the issued share capital for which cash has been requested. A company is not bound to call up all its issued share capital at once.

(d) *Paid-up share capital.* This refers to that part of the called-up share capital for which payment has been received.

(e) *Uncalled share capital.* This refers to that part of the issued share capital which has not been called up.

(f) *Unissued share capital.* This refers to that part of the authorized share capital which has not been allotted to members.

Shares

A share is a fixed unit of a limited company's capital. It may also be said to be a measure of an investor's interest and his liability within a company. For instance, if an individual purchases ten one-pound shares in a company then his investment is ten pounds and his liability, in the event of the company suffering financial difficulties, is limited to his ten pound investment.

Shares are divided into three main classes:
Preference,
Ordinary,
Deferred.

(a) *Preference shares.* These normally have the first claim to a fixed non-cumulative dividend on current profits available for distribution. They also usually have prior claim of capital repayments in the case of a company winding-up.

(b) *Cumulative preference shares.* These are similar to preference shares with an additional advantage to the investor in the sense that dividends not paid to the holder in one year accumulate until the company can afford to pay.

(c) *Participating preference shares.* Again, these are similar to preference shares plus the additional benefit of participating in surplus profits (if available) after the ordinary shareholders have received a dividend.

(d) *Redeemable preference shares.* These may be non-cumulative, cumulative or participating. A company issuing such shares may, at a future date, redeem them, either out of profits or out of the proceeds of a fresh issue of shares. These shares may not be redeemed unless they are fully paid.

(e) *Ordinary shares.* Dividends are paid on these shares after the preference share dividends have been met. The ordinary share capital of a company is termed 'equity' or 'risk' capital. The fortunes of these shareholders usually fluctuate with profit earned by a company, but they normally hold the voting control of a company.

(f) *Deferred or founders' shares.* Dividends are not declared on these shares until the entitlements of the preference and ordinary shareholders have been met. They tend, in practice, to be obtained by the promoters or founders of a company and sometimes by the vendors of a company.

Debentures

A debenture is a loan, therefore it follows that a debenture bond is a company's acknowledgement of a loan. A debenture holder is not a member (proprietor) of a company but simply a creditor, who is paid interest (normally half-yearly) which must be met even if the company sustains a loss. A shareholder (proprietor) may only receive a part dividend, in lean years, or no dividend at all.

As in the case of shares, debentures may be redeemable on or before a certain date, irredeemable or convertible. A convertible debenture is one which is issued to the public with the right (on certain terms), at a future date, to convert into ordinary shares.

Debentures may be 'naked' or 'secured'. If 'naked' then the company only undertakes to repay the loan without offering security. In the case of 'secured' (mortgage) debentures, then the company undertaking to repay a loan is secured by a charge on certain of its assets (termed a 'fixed charge') or the business as a whole (termed a 'floating charge').

Fairly frequently companies issue debentures as collateral security for bank loans and overdrafts. Collateral security is a secondary security and normally applies to the rendering of documents, e.g. debenture bonds, conveying the right to assets, e.g. cash, investments, property, etc., so that in the event of failure to settle a loan or other liability, there may be at least some benefit available to the lender without the necessity to embark on legal proceedings.

Accounting treatment of shares and debentures

The manner in which shares and debentures are issued and

recorded in the accounts is similar in both cases. Exhibits 13–1 to 13–3 illustrate the issuing of shares and debentures and the effect on the balance sheet of a company.

Exhibit 13–1 Issue of shares and debentures – payable in full.

A company issued 40,000 6% preference shares of £1 each, 20,000 ordinary shares of £1 each and 500 7% debentures bonds of £20 each. These were all subscribed and fully paid up.

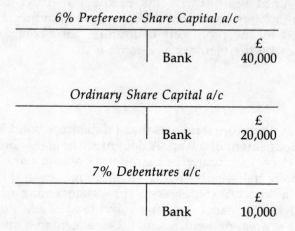

6% Preference Share Capital a/c

		£
	Bank	40,000

Ordinary Share Capital a/c

		£
	Bank	20,000

7% Debentures a/c

		£
	Bank	10,000

Clearly double entry is completed by debiting the bank account in the cash book.

Balance Sheet

	£		£
Issued Share Capital			
40,000 6% preference shares of £1 each fully paid	40,000		
20,000 ordinary shares of £1 each fully paid	20,000		
Long-Term Liabilities			
500 7% debentures of £20 each	10,000	Cash at bank	70,000
	70,000		70,000

Exhibit 13–2 Issues of shares and debentures at a premium.

A company issued 10,000 ordinary shares of £1 each at £1.20 each and 100 7½% debentures of £50 each at a premium of 10%. These were all subscribed and fully paid.

Ordinary Share Capital a/c

		£
	Bank	10,000

Share Premium a/c

		£
	Bank	2,000

7½% Debentures a/c

		£
	Bank	5,000

Debenture Premium a/c

		£
	Bank	500

Balance Sheet

	£		£
Issued Share Capital			
10,000 ordinary shares of £1 each, fully paid	10,000		
Reserves			
Share premium a/c	2,000		
Debenture premium a/c	500		
Long-Term Liabilities			
100 7½% debentures of £50 each	5,000	Cash at bank	17,500
	17,500		17,500

Exhibit 13–3 Issue of shares and debentures at a discount.

A company issued 5,000 6½% preference shares of £1 each at £0.95 and 300 5% debentures bonds of £10 each at a discount of 6%. These were all subscribed and fully paid.

6½% Preference Share Capital a/c

		£
	Bank	4,750
	Share discount a/c	250

Share Discount a/c

	£	
6½% preference share capital a/c	250	

5% Debentures a/c

			£
		Bank	2,820
		Debenture discount a/c	180

Debenture Discount a/c

	£	
5% debenture a/c	180	

Balance Sheet

Issued Share Capital	£		£
5,000 6½% preference shares of £1 each fully paid	5,000		
Long-Term Liabilities		Cash at bank	7,570
300 5% debentures of £10 each fully paid	3,000	Share discount	250
		Debenture discount	180
	8,000		8,000

Provisions and reserves

The Companies Act 1985 defines a provision as 'any amount written off or retained by way of providing for depreciation, renewal or diminution in the value of assets or retained by way of providing for any known liability of which the amount cannot be determined with substantial accuracy'. The Act does not directly define a reserve but states, in other words, that a reserve is not a provision.

The provisions for depreciation, renewals, etc., are fairly straightforward and have been dealt with in Chapter 9, but the second kind, i.e. for a known liability etc., is not so clear. However, company corporation tax (discussed below) is an example and the setting up of a provision for deferred repairs another.

Reserves are fundamentally divided into capital and revenue. Capital reserve examples are premiums received on issuing shares, profits set aside for redeeming shares, and so on, these being amounts which are not allowed to be used wholly or partly for distribution in the form of dividends. Revenue reserves, e.g. general reserve and balance of undistributed profits, are available, if so decided, as dividends.

To assist in deciding whether a particular item is, for legal purposes, a provision or reserve the following are considered reasonable in accounting circles:

(a) provisions are debited to the profit and loss account;

(b) reserves are debited to the profit and loss appropriation account;

(c) reserves are free and not intended to meet any contingencies, liabilities or losses known to exist at the date of the balance sheet;

(d) provisions may be for specific items existing at the date of the balance sheet which cannot be substantially estimated.

Corporation tax

United Kingdom corporation tax is applicable to limited companies. Sole traders and partnerships remain liable to income tax. Corporation tax is assessed on the profits* arising in a company's accounting period. The rate of tax is normally announced in the annual budget and relates to the previous financial year 1st April–31st March. In practice, the figure of net profit to be found in the profit and loss account is unlikely to be the amount on which corporation tax is assessable. This is because certain adjustments are usually necessary to arrive at the profit figure assessable for corporation tax purposes. One such adjustment is depreciation of fixed assets. Depreciation itself is not allowable for corporation tax purposes and is therefore added back to net profit. However, the Inland Revenue does make allowances for depreciation in the form of 'capital allowances' which may be deductible from profits.

Advance corporation tax (ACT)

When a company resident in the United Kingdom pays a dividend it will be liable to make an advance payment of corporation tax** calculated by reference to that distribution at the rate in force for the financial year in which the distribution is made. If the rate of ACT for the financial year 1984/85 was 33⅓% on the gross dividend, then if a company paid a dividend on 30th June 1984 of £15,000 it will be liable to account for ACT of ⅓ × £15,000 = £5,000. The gross dividend plus ACT is described as a 'franked payment' which in the example is £20,000. If the recipient of a dividend is a company resident in the United Kingdom the amount of value of the dividend together with a tax credit for the ACT is known as 'franked investment income'. Such income is not liable to corporation tax by

---

* Profits for corporation tax purposes comprise income and capital gains.

** For further reading on advance corporation tax, refer to the end of this chapter.

the receiving company. Subject to certain limitations, any ACT paid in respect of dividends made in an accounting period may be set-off against the corporation tax on income of that period, so reducing the total corporation tax liability.

Exhibit 13–4 is an example of how the set-off ACT operates, so as to reduce a company's mainstream corporation tax liability.

Exhibit 13–4

In the year to 31st March 1985 a company has a profit assessable for corporation tax of £100,000 and pay dividends of £30,000 in that year. Assume a corporation tax rate of 50% and an ACT rate of 33⅓%.

		£	£
ACT	£30,000 × 33⅓%		10,000
Corporation tax liability £100,000 × 50%		50,000	
Less: ACT		10,000	
Mainstream corporation tax payable at due date:			40,000
Total corporation tax paid:			50,000

The shareholders resident in the United Kingdom receive £30,000 together with a tax credit of £10,000.

Accounting treatment of corporation tax

Exhibit 13–5 illustrates how corporation tax* may be treated in the accounts of limited companies.

Exhibit 13–5

A limited company prepares its annual accounts on 31st December. For the year ended 31st December 1984 its liability for corporation tax on that year's profits was estimated at £10,250. On 30th September 1985 the corporation tax liability on the previous year's profits was agreed at £10,100. The corporation tax liability in respect of profits for the year ended 31st December 1985 was estimated to be at £12,500. Corporation tax for the previous year's profits is payable on 1st January each year. All tax payments were made on the due dates.

* For the sake of simplicity ACT has been completely ignored in respect of this and all other limited company accounts examples.

Corporation Tax a/c

1984		£	1984		£
Dec.31 Balance c/d		10,250	Dec.31 Profit and loss a/c		10,250
		10,250			10,250
1985			1985		
Dec.31 Profit and loss a/c		150	Jan. 1 Balance b/d		10,250
	Balance b/d	22,600	Dec.31 Profit and loss a/c		12,500
		22,750			22,750
1986			1986		
Jan. 1 Bank		10,100	Jan. Balance b/d		10,100
					12,500

Profit and Loss Account (extract) for year ended 31st Dec. 1984		Balance Sheet (extract) 31st Dec. 1984	
			£
Corporation tax £10,250		Provision for corporation tax	10,250

Profit and Loss Account (extract) for year ended 31st Dec. 1985		Balance Sheet (extract) 31st Dec. 1985	
			£
Corporation tax £12,500	Over provision of tax £150	Provision for corporation tax	12,500
		Current liabilities Corporation tax	10,100

It may be seen in Exhibit 13–5 above, that the amount of corporation tax payable at the end of a period is estimated and charged to that period. The following year when the figure is agreed by the Inland Revenue, then an adjustment is effected in that year, i.e. an overprovision being a credit (increasing net profit) in the profit and loss account, as in the above case, and an underprovision being debited (decreasing net profit) therein. The balance sheet extracts illustrate that a current year's corporation tax estimate (after adjustment) is shown as a current liability.

Profit and loss appropriation account

Fundamentally, the profit and loss appropriation account of a limited company is where net profit, after providing for taxation, is divided.

To net profit after tax is added the balance of the previous year's unappropriated profits (if a credit balance) and any over-provision of taxation attributable thereto. The various appropriations are then deducted from the resulting figure. These include transfers to reserves* and any dividends whether proposed or already paid. The balance is carried forward to the next year. This balance is listed under reserves in the balance sheet.

Exhibit 13–6

An example of a company's profit and loss account is illustrated in vertical form, below:

Profit and Loss Appropriation Account
for year ended 31st December 1986

	£	£
NET PROFITS after tax		70,000
Unappropriated profit b/f from previous year	7,700	
Overprovision of tax from previous year	300	8,000
		78,000
Less: Appropriations		
10% Debenture redemption reserve fund	6,000	
General reserve	9,000	
Dividends (Gross):		
Paid: 8% Preference share	8,000	
Ordinary Share (4%)	16,000	
Proposed:		
Ordinary Share (6%)	24,000	
		63,000
Unappropriated profits c/f to next year		15,000

Balance sheet

Having considered the capital, reserve and loan structures of limited companies it is important to observe the order in which they, and their component parts, are arranged on a balance sheet. This is demonstrated in Exhibit 13–7.

* Examples being preference share or debenture redemption reserve (sinking) fund and general reserve.

Exhibit 13–7

Illustrated below in vertical form is an example of a limited company balance sheet.

Balance Sheet as at 31st December 1986

Fixed Assets	Cost £	Depr. £	Net £
Freehold premises	569,000	–	569,000
Furniture and equipment	103,500	30,000	73,500
	672,500	30,000	642,500
Current Assets			
Stocks	34,000		
Debtors	29,000		
Bank and cash	9,500		
		72,500	
Less: Current Liabilities			
Creditors	13,000		
Corporation tax (on previous year's profits)	30,000		
Proposed dividends:			
6% on ordinary shares	24,000		
		67,000	
Working Capital			5,500
Capital Employed			648,000

FINANCED BY:	Auth. £	Issued £
Share Capital		
100,000 8% Preference shares of £1 each, fully paid	100,000	100,000
400,000 Ordinary shares of £1 each, fully paid	400,000	400,000
	500,000	500,000
Reserves		
Share premium	10,000	
10% Debenture redemption reserve fund	6,000	
General reserve	62,000	
Unappropriated profit c/f	15,000	
		93,000
SHAREHOLDERS' FUNDS/INVESTMENT		593,000
10% Debentures	20,000	
Future corporation tax (on current year's profits)	35,000	55,000
		648,000

It will be observed that the paid dividends do not appear in the balance sheet as the liability to pay has been discharged by the payment itself.

Questions and problems

13–1 What do you understand by 'the principle of limited liability'?

13–2 Describe the difference between the capital structure of a sole trader and a limited company.

13–3 How is it possible that the authorized and issued share capital of one company may be the same amount whereas in another company there may be a considerable disparity between the two?

13–4 Compare and contrast shares and debentures.

13–5 An hotel company transacted the following:
   (a) 15,000 ordinary shares of £1 each at a premium of £0.15; and
   (b) 5,000 9% debentures of £5 each at a discount of £0.20.
   Show the appropriate extracts in the company's balance sheet.

13–6 Smart Service Co. Ltd has an authorized share capital of £150,000 comprising 50,000 preference shares of £1 each issued and fully paid and £100,000 ordinary shares of £1 each of which 50,000 are issued and fully paid.
   The details below relate to the company on 31st January 1987:

	£
General reserve	12,000
Current assets	28,000
Current liabilities	22,000
Fixed assets	190,000
Unappropriated profit	10,000
Provision for depreciation on fixed assets	20,000
11% Debenture	54,000

Draft a summarized balance sheet for the company as at 31st January 1987, indicating shareholders' funds, working capital and capital employed.

13-7 The following trial balance was extracted from the records of Fishers Restaurants Ltd as at 28th February 1987:

	£000	£000
Authorized and issued share capital:		
500,000 ordinary shares of £1 each		500
Directors' remuneration	50	
Retained profit b/f 29th February 1986		17
Debtors and creditors	22	26
Wages and salaries	110	
Provision for depreciation on equipment to 29th		
February 1986		5
Equipment, at cost	24	
Freehold land and buildings, at cost	510	
Stocks of food and beverages	13	
Repairs and renovations	7	
Purchases and sales	180	420
Administration	10	
Laundry	4	
Rates and insurances	12	
Cash in hand	3	
Balance at bank	25	
Advance booking deposits		2
	970	970

The following information is relevant:
(a) Stocks of food and beverages at 28.2.87, £16,000.
(b) Provision for depreciation on equipment is to be made at the rate of 10% per annum using the straight line method.
(c) Rates and insurances paid in advance at 28.2.87, £4,000.
(d) Provide for a dividend of 10%.
You are required to prepare a trading, profit and loss account for the year ended 28th February 1987, and a balance sheet as at that date.

13-8 The Midville Catering Co. Ltd commenced business on 1st April 1985. Its authorized capital was 50,000 ordinary shares of £1 each and 50,000 5% preference shares of £1 each. The company has issued 50,000 of each class of share and these are fully paid up. From the following trial balance extracted from the books of the company after the preparation of the trading account, you are required to prepare a profit and loss account for the year ended 31st March 1987, and a balance sheet as at that date.

	£	£
Ordinary share capital		50,000
5% Preference share capital		50,000
6% Debentures		20,000
Share premium account		5,000
Gross profit		35,405
Directors' fees	3,000	
Auditors' fees	500	
Administrative expenses	10,000	
Selling expenses	4,000	
Other expenses	2,000	
6% Debenture interest (6 months)	600	
Preliminary expenses	1,800	
Discounts received		450
Dividends received		200
Discounts allowed	150	
Sundry debtors	4,500	
Sundry creditors		6,000
Cash at bank	3,655	
Stock in trade	9,000	
Fixed assets, at cost		
Catering premises	87,600	
Furnishings	22,000	
Equipment	12,000	
Linen	6,500	
Advanced booking deposit		250
	167,305	167,305

Take into account the following adjustments:

(a) Depreciate all fixed assets, except premises at 10% per annum on cost.
(b) Accrued administration expenses are £80.
(c) Prepaid other expenses are £75.
(d) Provide £450 against bad debts.
(e) Provide £4,000 for corporation tax, payable 1st January 1987
(f) Provide for a dividend of 5% on ordinary shares.
(g) Transfer £1,500 to general reserve.
(h) Allow for a further 6 months' debenture interest.

13–9 The following balances have been extracted from the books of the Mistan Company Limited as at 30th September 1986:

	£
Creditors	12,600
Sales	160,000
Land at cost	36,000
Buildings at cost	76,000
Furniture and fittings at cost	44,000
Bank (credit balance)	12,000
Depreciation – buildings	12,000
– furniture and fittings	20,000
Discounts received	3,528
Unappropriated profit at 1 October 1985	4,000
Provision for doubtful debts	1,632
Goodwill	32,800
Cash in hand	464
Stock at 1 October 1985	28,496
Interim dividend on preference shares	1,200
Rates	4,248
Wages and salaries	16,000
Insurance	3,792
Allowances	744
General expenses	872
Debtors	25,280
Purchases	87,712
Debenture interest	800
Bad debts	1,352
5% Debentures	32,000
6% £1 Preference shares	40,000
£1 Ordinary shares	40,000
General reserve	20,000
Share premium	2,000

Additional information:

(a) Stock on hand at 30 September 1986 was £31,092.
(b) Insurance paid in advance – £200.
(c) Wages owing – £560.
(d) Depreciation is to be provided at 10% on cost of buildings, and at 20% on the written down value of furniture and fittings.
(e) Provision for doubtful debts is to be reduced to 5% of debtors.
(f) Debenture interest outstanding of £800.
(g) The directors propose to pay a 5% ordinary dividend and the final preference dividend, and to transfer £16,000 to general reserve.

Required:
Prepare the trading, profit and loss and appropriation

account for the period ended 30th September 1986 and a balance sheet as at that date.

Further reading

1. *Corporation Tax* (IR 18) Inland Revenue, HMSO.
2. Wood, F., *Business Accounting* (Vol. II) Pitman Publishing Ltd (1984); Chapters 34 to 42.
3. Williams, R. G., *Comprehensive Aspects of Taxation* (Revised by B. Mendes), Donnington Press.

Chapter Fourteen
Departmental Accounting

It has been seen so far that the trading results of a business have been determined by calculating the overall profit or loss obtained. However, although this may prove sufficient for the smaller concern, the management of a medium or larger business will normally require to know, in addition to the overall result, the profit or loss made in each department.

The degree of departmentalization is dependent on the size of a business and the judgement of its management. The basic departments in hotel and catering establishments comprise commodity sales:

Rooms
Food
Liquor   } Commodity sales
Tobacco
Other income

By analysing income and expenditure into the above departments management may ascertain the trading result of each commodity. If a greater degree of departmentalization is required then the business may be segregated into points of sale. For instance, in the case of an hotel with two restaurants and one bar the following may apply:

Rooms
Restaurant 1
Restaurant 2   } Points of sale
Bar
Other income

In this case, to obtain a trading result for each department (point of sale) food would be requisitioned for each restaurant from a central store, and so on for liquor and tobacco, thus enabling each departmental sales point's profit or loss to be determined.

Departmental book-keeping

Departmental recording may principally be achieved by analysing the relevant day books. By way of illustration 'purchases' are considered below in Exhibit 14–1.

Exhibit 14–1

Purchases Day Book

				Total	Food	Liquor	Tobacco

The purchases returns book will have a similar ruling to the purchases day book but the sales day book will require an additional analysis column for room sales.

The analysed day book totals are either posted to analysed accounts, i.e. purchases, sales, etc., or to individual accounts, i.e. food purchases account, food sales account, etc., as required.

Profit levels

With the implementation of a complete departmental accounting system three profit levels may be attained. These are explained below.

(a) *Departmental gross profit.* This figure is obtained by the allocation of purchases, sales and stocks, allowing the gross profits of each commodity/point of sale to be obtained.

(b) *Departmental profit.* To obtain this figure, costs which are controllable by the department, i.e. wages and staff costs, laundry, etc., are deducted from the departmental gross profits. By introducing this intermediary profit calculation, a control may be maintained on expenses which are directly controlled by the departmental manager. Hence targets may be set, in the form of budgets,* inducing the departmental manager to ensure a tight rein is kept on his expenditure.

* Explained in Chapter 6, Vol. 2.

(c) *Departmental net profit*. This figure, although rarely ascertained, is determined by the reasonable but nevertheless arbitrary allotment of general running expenses which cannot, in normal circumstances, be controlled by departmental management. For example, it would be a gross misjudgement to apportion building insurance to each department to determine departmental net profit, when it is unlikely that departmental managers would be consulted on such matters.

In the practical situation the analysis of costs is an expensive task, therefore, it will normally be found that businesses tend to restrict their analyses to determining either departmental gross profit or departmental profit. Exhibit 14–2 is an example illustrating the departmental profit and loss account.

Exhibit 14–2

Trading, Profit and Loss Account
for period ended 31st December 1986

	Rooms £	Food £	Liquor and Tobacco £	Total £
Sales	20,000	24,000	8,000	52,000
Less: Cost of goods sold	–	10,000	4,500	14,500
DEPARTMENTAL GROSS PROFITS	20,000	14,000	3,500	37,500
Less: Departmental expenses				
Wages and staff costs	4,000	3,000	900	7,900
Laundry	1,700	1,200	200	3,100
Kitchen fuel		250		250
Glass and china		400	150	550
Other expenses	2,500	500	300	3,300
	8,200	5,350	1,550	15,100
DEPARTMENTAL PROFITS	11,800	8,650	1,950	22,400
Add: Other income				
Discount received				100
Investment income				400
				22,900

Less: Unapportioned expenses

Administration expenses	9,000
Repairs and maintenance	3,000
Depreciation	4,000
Heating and lighting	2,500
Advertising	400
Rates and insurances	1,000
Other expenses	200
	20,100
NET PROFIT for the period	2,800

Departmental accounts may be produced in various forms. An alternative presentation, using the same figures as in Exhibit 14–2, is set out in Exhibit 14–3.

Exhibit 14–3

Trading, Profit and Loss Account
for period ended 31st December 1986

	Sales £	Cost of Goods Sold £	Gross Profit £	Dept. Expenses £	Dept. Profit £
Rooms	20,000	–	20,000	8,200	11,800
Food	24,000	10,000	14,000	5,350	8,650
Liquor and tobacco	8,000	4,500	3,500	1,500	1,950
	52,000	14,500	37,500	15,100	22,400

Add: Other income

Discount received	100	
Investment income	400	
		500
		22,900

Less: Unapportioned expenses

Administration expenses	9,000	
Repairs and maintenance	3,000	
Depreciation	4,000	
Heating and lighting	2,500	
Advertising	400	
Rates and insurance	1,000	
Other expenses	200	
		20,100
NET PROFIT for the period		2,800

Allocation and apportionment

If a business wishes to obtain a departmental net profit then its remaining income and expenses will require to be allocated and apportioned. After each expense has been allocated as far as possible, for instance allocated to rooms, then the balance needs to be apportioned. Suggested bases will be according to the particular expense. For example, the unallocated repairs and maintenance may be apportioned to departments on the basis of turnover. Other bases of apportionment may be square feet, cubic feet, direct departmental wages and cost of goods sold.

Departmental net profit may be attained for both commodity departments and point of sale departments, although the latter figures obtained produce a more accurate result as more allocation and less apportionment of expenses is possible.

Questions and problems

14–1 Write brief notes explaining the difference between 'commodity sales' and 'point of sale' systems of departmental accounting.

14–2 What do you understand by the term 'profit level'? Name the three profit levels obtainable by maintaining a departmental accounting system and explain how each is achieved.

14–3 From the following information you are required to prepare the Half-Acre Hotel's trading and profit and loss account for the period ended 30th June 1985.

			£
Net sales:			
Rooms			8,000
Liquor and tobacco			25,300
Food			11,800
Net purchases:			
Food			5,600
Liquor and tobacco			13,500
Stocks	1st July 1984	30th June 1985	
	£	£	
Food	300	400	
Liquor and tobacco	1,200	950	
Wages and staff costs			15,100
Rates and insurance			2,750
Depreciation			3,400
General expenses			1,700

14-4 Compile a trading and profit and loss account from the details set out below showing the maximum amount of information possible:

	£
Turnover for the period:	
Rooms	70,000
Food	55,900
Liquor and tobacco	42,500
Other income	5,200
Purchases for the period:	
Food	21,700
Liquor and tobacco	24,650
Stocks at beginning of the period:	
Food	870
Liquor and tobacco	3,460
Stocks at end of the period:	
Food	1,100
Liquor and tobacco	4,000
Wages PAYE, etc., for the period:	
Rooms	6,150
Food	15,740
Liquor and tobacco	8,490
China, glass and linen consumed during the period:	
Rooms	1,400
Food	2,060
Liquor and tobacco	1,850
Heat, light and power for the period:	
Kitchen	430
General	1,810
Repairs and maintenance	12,200
Depreciation	7,500
Administration expenses	5,450
Sales advertising and promotion	3,800
Rates	9,000
Sundry other expenses	7,150

14-5 The Blue Motel has two revenue-producing departments, A and B. The following information relates to the Motel's trading during 1986:

	Dept. A £	Dept. B £	Total £
Purchases	40,000	60,000	100,000
Stocks: 1st Jan. 1986	2,500	4,000	6,500
31st Dec. 1986	3,500	5,000	8,500
Sales	100,000	120,000	220,000
Wages and salaries	22,500	37,500	60,000
Heat, light and power	2,100	3,250	5,350
Repairs and maintenance	–	–	12,000

Administration expenses	–	–	9,000
Rent and rates	–	–	10,000
Investment income	–	–	2,000
Depreciation	–	–	6,000
Loan interest	–	–	19,000
Advertising	–	–	4,750
Laundry expenses	–	–	3,300
Legal fees	–	–	1,000

Allocation and appointment of expenses:

1. Repairs and maintenance are apportioned in proportion to wages and salaries.
2. Of the management salaries £4,000 is allocated to Dept. A and £7,000 to Dept. B.
3. Laundry expenses are apportioned in proportion to sales.

You are required to prepare a departmental profit and loss statement for year ended 31st December 1986 indicating clearly:

(a) the gross profit and loss of each department;
(b) the departmental profit and loss of each department;
(c) the overall net profit or loss of the business.

14–6 The Crooked Bullet Ltd is a licensed restaurant which provides luncheons and evening meals. The trial balance for the business for the year 31st March 1985 was as follows:

	£	£
Freehold property at cost	80,000	
Equipment at cost	22,000	
Provision for depreciation – equipment		6,500
Stock at 1st April 1984 (see note (a))	4,600	
Purchases (see note (a))	123,000	
Sales (see note (a))		260,000
Wages	85,000	
Overhead expenses	40,600	
Authorized and issued £1 Ord. shares		80,000
Trade debtors	800	
Cash book	11,000	
Trade creditors		11,900
Unappropriated profit		8,600
	367,000	367,000

Additional information:
(a) The analysis of stock, purchases and sales was:

	Stock £	Purchases £	Sales £
Cigarettes	900	11,100	12,000
Beverages	2,500	16,600	49,600
Food	1,200	95,300	198,400
	4,600	123,000	260,000

(b) Closing stocks were:

Cigarettes	£1,200
Beverages	£3,000
Foods	£1,500
	£5,700

(c) Depreciation is to be charged at 10% on the straight-line method.

(d) Food included in stock which had been bought on credit for £250 had not been recorded in the ledgers.

(e) The company proposed to pay a dividend of £3,350.

You are required to:
(i) Prepare the trading accounts, a profit and loss account for the year ended 31st March 1985 and a balance sheet at that date.
(ii) Explain, if the gross profit percentage on sales of cigarettes should have been 11.5%, how the difference between that figure and the percentage shown in your trading account could have occurred. Indicate the amounts of cash or stock that could have been involved.

(*Ignore taxation*)   (HCIMA)

Chapter 15
Cost–Volume–Profit Relationships

Cost behaviour

Until now, cost has been considered in its basic elements of materials (e.g. food), labour (e.g. wages), and expenses (e.g. laundry and rates). This is, of course, a convenient way of classifying costs to give gross profit and net profit in the profit statement. For decision-making purposes, cost should also be considered from the point of view of how it responds to various influences.

Cost may be classified into materials, labour and expenses and these constitute the 'total cost' of a business. It is also possible to classify the same total cost by the way it behaves, namely *variable*, *semi-variable* and *fixed*.

A variable cost is one which in total tends to change *directly in proportion* to the level of activity, e.g. food, drink and casual labour. For instance, if the food cost of a certain dish is £1 then the cost of producing 100 would be £100 and 1,000 would be £1,000 and so on. The variable cost of one unit of a product or service, i.e. a cost which would be avoided if the unit was not produced or provided, is termed the 'marginal' cost.

A fixed cost may be said to be one which, *within limits*, does not vary with the level of activity, e.g. salaries, rates and insurance. For example, take the case of a manager who is paid an annual salary of £15,000. Even if he manages to increase sales by, say, 20% his salary will remain the same figure.

A semi-variable (or semi-fixed) cost is one which moves *in sympathy* with a change in the level of activity but *not* in proportion to wages, laundry, gas, electricity and so on. Take the case of gas. If double the number of meals are sold, the gas bill *will* increase but the cost *will not* double.

For certain cost–volume–profit analysis only variable and fixed costs are included, the semi-variable costs being divided into their variable and fixed elements. Separation may be achieved by technical, graphical or mathematical means (discussed in Chapter 5, Vol. 2).

Exhibit 15–1 gives in diagrammatic form the explanation so far.

Exhibit 15–1

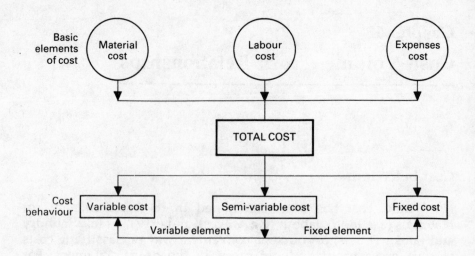

It is now appropriate to illustrate the variable and fixed costs graphically (see Exhibit 15–2). The graphs depict activity on the horizontal scales of 20,000 units (meals) and value, in the form of sales and costs, on the vertical scales. Notice, for example, that at 10,000 and 15,000 meals the variable costs are £10,000 and £15,000 respectively, whereas the fixed cost remains at £10,000 at both levels.

Exhibit 15–2

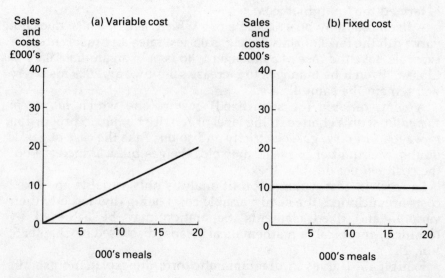

Break-even graph

Variable costs plus fixed costs equal total cost. If the two costs are combined on a single graph, then they will appear as in Exhibit 15–3.

Exhibit 15–3

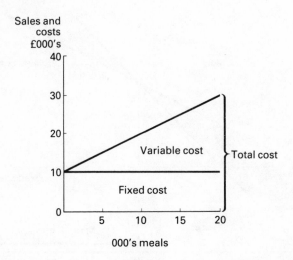

By introducing a sales revenue line a break-even graph is formed as shown in Exhibit 15–4

From this graph a firm's 'break-even point' (BEP) may be read, i.e. that point at which neither a profit is made nor a loss sustained. At this point total cost is equal to total revenue. Further observation will reveal that profit and/or losses may be read off the graph at various levels of activity. For instance, at 5,000 meals a £5,000 (£15,000 − £10,000) loss is incurred, whereas at 20,000 meals a £10,000 (£40,000 − £30,000) profit is achieved. Note also that the difference between the budgeted number of meal sales and the break-even point is known as the 'margin of safety', which in this example is 10,000 meals, i.e. 20,000 − 10,000 meals.

Exhibit 15–4 Break-even graph

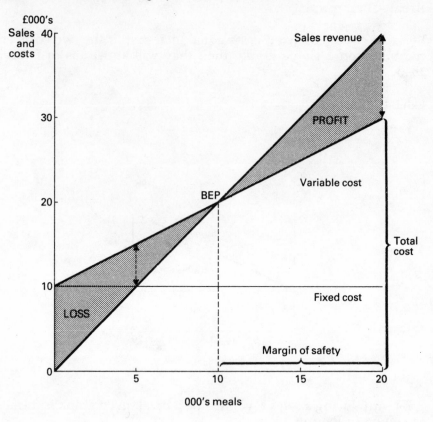

Contribution break-even graph

If the two cost lines in the break-even graph shown in Exhibit 15–4 are reversed then a 'contribution break-even graph' is established as in Exhibit 15–5.

This graph contains all the detail and information included in the previous break-even graph. It does, however, reveal an additional feature highlighted by the shaded area, known as the 'contribution margin'.

Contribution margin concept

Closer observation of the graph in Exhibit 15–5 will disclose that the contribution margin is the difference between the *sales revenue* and *variable cost*. If the graph is translated into a financial statement then the following 'total' column will result (see opposite):

Exhibit 15–5 Contribution break-even graph

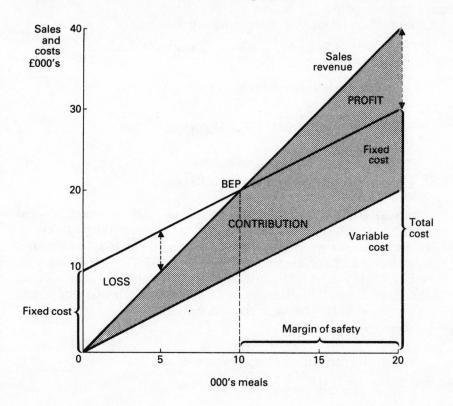

Exhibit 15–6 Marginal cost statement

	Total	Per unit	% Relationship
Volume of meals	20,000		
	£	£	%
Sales	40,000	2.00	100
Less: Variable cost	20,000	1.00	50
Contribution margin	20,000	1.00	50
Less: Fixed cost	10,000		
Net profit	10,000		

It will be appreciated that the statement has been prepared for an assumed maximum level of activity of 20,000 meals. A swift check against the contribution break-even graph will confirm that at

20,000 meals sales are £40,000, contribution is £20,000 and fixed costs and net profit are both £10,000.

Expressed in terms of a simple equation:

Contribution margin = Sales − Variable costs

or

Contribution margin = Fixed costs + Net profit

∴

Sales − Variable costs = Fixed costs + Profit

Calculating break-even, profit and loss

If alongside the above statement the selling price and variable cost per unit are determined, as above, then it becomes possible to calculate the break-even point. Every meal sold yields a contribution margin towards fixed cost of £1, therefore if 10,000 meals are sold then £10,000 worth of contribution margin is achieved and is equal to the fixed costs. This then results in neither a profit nor a loss (break-even point). The formula and figures are:

$$\text{BEP} = \frac{\text{Fixed cost}}{\text{Contribution margin per unit}}$$

$$= \frac{£10,000}{£1}$$

$$= \underline{10,000} \text{ units (meals)}$$

A check against either foregone graphs will verify the result.

Commercial organizations, such as hotels and restaurants, need to make a profit. If then the same example is developed, every meal above 10,000 that is sold provides a contribution margin of £1. Assuming the required profit is £10,000 then the formula will be:

$$\text{Profit required} = \frac{\text{Fixed cost + Profit}}{\text{Contribution margin per unit}}$$

$$= \frac{£10,000 + £10,000}{£1}$$

$$= \underline{20,000} \text{ units (meals)}$$

Again a brief check against the break-even charts will confirm the answer.

Finally, what of the non-commercial organizations such as universities, hospitals and school meals which *subsidize* eating facilities of students, staff and pupils? Again, all that is required is that the basic BEP formula is modified. Still referring to the above example, assume that instead of a profit being required a loss, in the form of a subsidy, of £2,000 is acceptable:

$$\text{Loss (subsidy) required} = \frac{\text{Fixed cost} - \text{loss}}{\text{Contribution margin per unit}}$$

$$= \frac{£10,000 - £2,000}{£1}$$

$$= \underline{8,000} \text{ units (meals)}$$

Reference to the graphs will indicate that if 8,000 meals are sold then a loss of £2,000 is sustained. In this context the loss was, of course, a planned subsidy.

Contribution margin to sales ratio

This ratio, previously known as the 'P/V ratio', refers to the % *relationship* column alongside the earlier statement. It is simply the relationship of contribution margin to sales expressed as a percentage and as such may be substituted for the contribution margin per unit in all the above formulae. The only difference in using the contribution to sales ratio arises out of the fact that the result is expressed in sales value *not* units (meals). Applying the above information the position will appear as follows:

$$\text{BEP} = \frac{\text{Fixed cost}}{\text{C/S ratio}}$$

$$= \frac{£10,000}{50\%}$$

$$= \frac{£10,000 \times 100}{50}$$

$$= \underline{£20,000} \text{ sales value}$$

$$\text{Profit required} = \frac{\text{Fixed cost} + \text{Profit}}{\text{C/S ratio}}$$

$$= \frac{£10,000 + £10,000}{50\%}$$

$$= \frac{£20,000 \times 100}{50}$$

$$= \underline{£40,000} \text{ sales value}$$

$$\text{Loss required} = \frac{\text{Fixed cost} - \text{loss}}{\text{C/S ratio}}$$

$$= \frac{£10,000 - £2,000}{50\%}$$

$$= \frac{£8,000 \times 100}{50}$$

$$= \underline{£16,000} \text{ sales value}$$

Example of cost–profit–volume analysis

Having covered the principles involved in cost–volume–profit relationships it is appropriate to consider an example. The budgeted details of two restaurant companies are as follows:

	Restaurant A	Restaurant B
Budgeted sales in units	10,000	10,000
Budgeted selling price per unit	£2.00	£2.00
Budgeted variable cost per unit	£1.50	£1.00
Budgeted fixed expenses total	£3,000	£8,000
Budgeted capacity	80%	80%

Compute for each company:
  (a) the budgeted profit;
  (b) the budgeted break-even point in units;
  (c) the impact on profits of a ±10% deviation in sales, and comment briefly on the effect of this in relation to the distribution between the company's fixed and variable expenses.

Solution

	A			B	
(a) Units	10,000	units		10,000	units
Sales	20,000	2.00		20,000	2.00
Less: Variable costs	15,000	1.50		10,000	1.00
CONTRIBUTION	5,000	0.50		10,000	1.00
Less: Fixed costs	3,000			8,000	
NET PROFIT	2,000			2,000	

(b) $\text{BEP} = \dfrac{\text{Fixed cost}}{\text{CM per unit}}: \quad \dfrac{£3,000}{£0.5} = \underline{6,000}\text{ units} \qquad \dfrac{£8,000}{£1} = \underline{8,000}\text{ units}$

(c) 10% sales deviation = 1,000 units
±10% sales deviation   = ±1,000 × £0.50   = ±1,000 × £1
                                        = ±£500   = ±£1,000

Comment on (c)

As by definition the fixed costs remain constant then the impact on contribution margin will be reflected in net profit. Restaurant B has a higher proportion of fixed costs to total costs than Restaurant A and as a result will experience a greater impact on profits from a similar deviation in sales.

It is worth mentioning that many hotels have cost structures which contain a high proportion of fixed costs, whereas institutional catering situations tend to have a lower proportion of fixed costs. (This topic is discussed further in Chapter 12, Vol. 2).

Application of cost–volume–profit analysis

Cost–volume–profit relationships are a most important aid in the decision-making process of management. Put more precisely, they assist managers to choose between alternative courses of action. To demonstrate this a case is illustrated.

Closing down a department

Below is the annual profit statement of a catering business which has three departments:

	Dept. 1 £	Dept. 2 £	Dept. 3 £	Total £
Sales	8,000	18,000	10,000	36,000
Less: Total costs				
Food	3,000	3,000	2,000	8,000
Direct labour	2,000	4,000	2,000	8,000
Variable overhead	1,000	2,000	1,000	4,000
Fixed overhead	3,000	3,000	2,000	8,000
	9,000	12,000	7,000	28,000
Net profit (loss)	(1,000)	6,000	3,000	8,000

Department 1 has consistently made losses and the company is considering closing it down.

	(A) Retain Dept. 1 £	(B) Close Dept. 1 £	(A) − (B) Difference £
Sales	36,000	28,000	8,000
Less: Variable costs	20,000	14,000	6,000
Contribution margin	16,000	14,000	2,000
Less: Fixed overhead	8,000	8,000	Nil
Net profit	8,000	6,000	2,000

If Department 1 is closed then net profit will fall by £2,000. This is due to the fact that the fixed overhead of £3,000 is still incurred but the positive contribution margin of £2,000 earned by the department will be foregone. Therefore, on financial grounds Department 1 should be retained.

Notes:
  (a) The allocation of fixed overhead between the three departments is simply arbitrary (a matter of opinion), i.e. one could argue that Department 1 should only suffer £1,500 of fixed overhead thereby turning a £1,000 loss into a £500 profit. In any event, unless otherwise indicated, the £3,000 fixed overhead would have to be borne by the other two departments.
  (b) A financial analysis that shows only the third column (A − B) is referred to as *differential* (or *incremental*) analysis.

Questions and problems

15–1 Distinguish between 'variable' and 'fixed' costs.

15–2 What is a semi-variable cost?

15–3 What do you understand by the term 'break-even point'?

15–4 Explain what is meant by the term 'contribution margin'.

15–5 What is the margin of safety?

15–6 Explain the contribution margin to sales ratio.

15–7 A new restaurant is being opened in the near future for which annual fixed costs are expected to be: rent £6,400, rates £1,200, salaries £8,800, depreciation 15% per annum on the cost of equipment and other costs £370. Variable costs (excluding food) are estimated to be 20% of sales.

It is the policy to add 200% to the food cost to give a selling price of £6 per cover.

Equipment costing £16,400 has been purchased.

From the above information you are required to determine by calculation the following:
  (a) the break-even point in number of covers per annum; and
  (b) the number of covers necessary per annum to achieve a net profit of £2,800 and £14,000.

15–8 The management of a 60 seat table d'hôte restaurant is considering its pricing and costing policies. Three possibilities are being considered:

  (i) Price of meal £9.20; food cost, 40% of net price; fixed costs £72,000; estimated demand, 20,000 meals.
  (ii) By providing rather more and better quality food at a cost of £3.80 a price of £11.50 might be set; fixed costs remain at £72,000; estimated demand, 15,000 meals.
  (iii) By improving decor, general amenity, and advertising, a price of £12.65 might be set for the meal described in (ii) above. These improvements would involve a long-term borrowing requirement of £40,000 at 20% interest, and an additional spending of £4,000 a year on advertising.

Note: The prices given are menu prices, that is, include VAT at 15%.

You are required to:
  (a) Calculate which of these policies will maximize profit.
  (b) Calculate the margin of safety and safety factor for each of these policies.
  (c) Considering all the relevant factors, state which policy would, in your view, be preferable overall, and why.
                                                              (HCIMA)

15–9 The budgeted sales of two companies are as follows.

	Company 1	Company 2
Budgeted sales in units	10,000	10,000
Budgeted selling price per unit	£2.00	£2.00
Budgeted variable costs per unit	£1.50	£1.00
Budgeted fixed expenses total	£3,000	£8,000

With respect to each company:

(a) Calculate:
   (i) budgeted net profit;
   (ii) break-even point;
   (iii) margin of safety.
(b) Prepare break-even charts.
(c) Show by calculation which company would make the most net profit if budgeted sales increased by 20%. Explain your results.

Chapter Sixteen
Introduction to Budgetary Control

Budgetary control contains two main elements:

(a) the establishment of budgets relating to the responsibility of executives and the requirements of policy;

(b) the continuous comparison of actual with budgeted results for the purpose of taking appropriate corrective action.

On the one side, therefore, it is concerned with planning, and on the other control. This chapter concentrates on the planning aspect of budgetary control.

Advantages of budgetary control

The benefits that can be obtained if budgets are administered with care and sensitivity are substantial. In particular budgets:

(a) give a business direction;

(b) compel management to plan;

(c) provide a basis on which to compare subsequent performance;

(d) encourage communication and teamwork between different parts of an organization.

Budget organization

The annual budget programme is organized and administered through a budget committee. The committee comprises senior managers of the organization who are responsible for major functions. In an hotel business the membership of the committee could comprise the general manager, deputy manager, food and beverage manager, front office manager, executive housekeeper and the accountant, who will normally act as secretary and budget co-ordinator.

The work of the budget committee usually consists of receiving and approving budgets submitted by departmental heads for the coming year, and subsequently reviewing performance. Where the committee consider particular budgets to be out of line with company policy, it may require them to be re-presented before approval is given. In the event of significant differences (or variances) occurring between actual and budgeted results, the committee may order an investigation to be undertaken to ascertain the reason for the variances and thus be in a position to recommend corrective measures to improve the situation in the future. At the end of the budget year the committee will review performance for the whole period and in the light of prevailing conditions, use the results as a guide to formulating policy for the following year.

The budget procedures will normally be set out in a budget manual which managers, who are responsible for budgets, can use as a source of reference.

Limiting factors

Limiting factors are determinants (or variables) which serve to constrain the operation or growth of a business. In general, these include numbers of customers, material, labour and capital availability. There is little point in (say) planning a major change in menu policy for the coming year if the supply of certain key ingredients is unreliable. Thus, prior to finalizing an annual budget adequate consideration should be given to all the factors that might adversely affect business operations.

An important limiting factor in the hotel and catering industry is capacity, i.e. bedrooms, seating, etc. Hotels have a fixed number of rooms which cannot be increased in the short term. Hence the number of rooms available during the year is a critical factor which should be taken into account in preparing the rooms revenue budget. It is important to remember that an unsold room during a period is revenue lost forever and therefore has an immediate effect on profit.

It has already been pointed out that material availability, i.e. food and beverages, may prove to be a limiting factor. Also, labour may be a limiting factor. For instance, there may not be sufficient potential employees available for work who have the right skills. This might result in the hotel budgeting for an increase in training facilities in order to ensure that new staff engaged are properly trained for the work required of them.

There are numerous other limiting factors such as the availability of capital to refurbish or extend existing facilities, the quality of management, suitable equipment for particular work and so on, all of which must be considered when planning operations.

Classification of budgets

Budgets are classified into two groups, namely operating budgets and capital budgets. Operating budgets are associated with the provision of products and services, i.e. materials, labour and sales, whereas capital budgets are concerned with the estimation of capital expenditure, i.e. equipment acquisition and the amounts tied-up in stocks, debtors and cash. Exhibit 16–1 shows the individual budgets which form the annual budget.

Exhibit 16–1 Classification of budgets

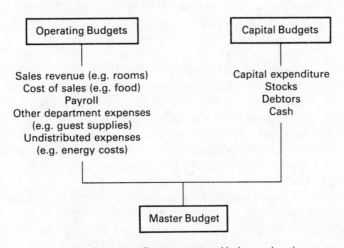

(Budgeted profit statement and balance sheet)

Notice that the operating budgets are combined to provide the budgeted profit statement for the year, and the capital budgets are combined to give the budgeted balance sheet at the year end. Together the two statements form the 'master budget'.

Sales forecasting

The most crucial budget is the sales revenue budget as all other budgets are based on the level of sales anticipated. For this reason the sales budget is sometimes referred to as the 'cornerstone of budgeting'.

Sales forecasting is a difficult task and therefore great care should be taken in preparation. Some of the factors that should be considered when forecasting sales revenue are given overleaf:

1. Past sales and sales mix
2. Advance bookings
3. Market studies
4. Capacity
5. Pricing policies
6. Sales promotion
7. Competition
8. Seasonal variations
9. Forthcoming events
10. Economic conditions

Cash budgeting

A business must have sufficient amounts of cash to meet day-to-day needs. If not, it will soon find that suppliers and other creditors are not prepared to provide materials and services.

A cash budget is a forecast of *receipts* and *payments* which is usually prepared on a weekly or monthly basis for the budget period. It should not be confused with the budgeted profit statement which is a forecast of *revenues* and *expenses*. The cash budget is primarily concerned with the *timing* of cash receipts and payments. A profit statement is a summary of revenues and expenses which have *accrued* during a period. This means that revenues and expenses are matched one with the other and dealt with in the profit statement of the period (year) to which they relate irrespective of the period that cash is received or paid out. The cash budget is prepared after all the other capital and operating budgets are prepared.

The cash budget provides a useful overview of the inflow and outflow of cash during the budget period. From this managers can be forewarned of likely shortfalls in cash during the year, such as peak periods, and make appropriate overdraft arrangements with the bank. It will also highlight periods with excessive cash surpluses so that the excess amounts can be invested in short-term marketable securities to earn a return.

An example of a cash budget is presented together with a master budget prepared from given data in Exhibit 16–2.

Budget preparation

The example which follows shows that for an existing business the procedure is to begin first with the present financial position as shown in the balance sheet, apply the given forecasts and prepare the budgeted statements. The assumed data of the Sands Restaurant is set out in Exhibit 16–2.

Exhibit 16–2

On 31st December 19X1 the Sands Restaurant balance sheet disclosed the following:

	£		£
Capital	50,000	Freehold property	30,000
Trade creditors	4,600	Equipment	12,500
		Stocks	9,200
		Debtors	2,000
		Cash at bank	900
	54,600		54,600

The following forecasts and information for the three months to 31st March 19X2 have been provided:

(a)

Month	Sales of food & beverages £	Purchases of food & beverages £	Wages and other expenses £	Depn. of equipment £
Jan.	16,000	9,000	8,000	200
Feb.	20,000	10,000	9,000	200
Mar.	24,000	8,000	11,000	200

(b) Gross profit on sales is an average of 60%.
(c) Half the sales are for cash, the balance being credit sales which are settled in the month after the date of the transaction.
(d) All the purchases are on credit and suppliers are paid in the month after the date of the transaction.
(e) Wages and other expenses are paid out monthly in cash.
(f) A loan of £5,000 has been granted and will be received on 1st February. The annual interest rate is 12% to be paid half-yearly in arrears.
(g) On 1st February catering equipment is to be acquired, the price of which will be £7,500. The existing equipment that the new equipment is to replace is in the balance sheet at £1,500 and the supplier has agreed to accept it for a part exchange value of £1,000.

Required:
   (i) prepare the monthly cash budget from January to March 19X2 inclusive;
   (ii) calculate the closing stock value; and
   (iii) prepare a budgeted profit statement for the quarter ending 31st March 19X2, and a budgeted balance sheet as at that date.

Sands Restaurant
Cash Budget for quarter ending 31st March 19X2

	Jan. £	Feb. £	Mar. £
Receipts:			
Sales: Credit	2,000	8,000	10,000
Cash	8,000	10,000	12,000
Loan		5,000	
	10,000	23,000	22,000
Payments:			
Purchases: Credit	4,600	9,000	10,000
Wages, etc.	8,000	9,000	11,000
Equipment		6,500	
	12,600	24,500	21,000
Opening balance	900	(1,700)	(3,200)
Surplus/(deficit)	(2,600)	(1,500)	1,000
Closing balance	(1,700)	(3,200)	(2,200)

Budgeted Profit Statement for quarter
ending 31st March 19X2

	£	£
Sales		60,000
Less: Cost of Sales		
Opening stock	9,200	
Purchases	27,000	
	36,200	
Less: Closing stock	12,200	24,000
GROSS PROFIT		36,000
Less Expenses:		
Wages and other expenses	28,000	
Depreciation	600	
Loan interest (12/100 × £5,000 × 1/6)	100	
Loss on sale of equipment (£1,500 − £1,000)	500	29,200
NET PROFIT		6,800

Budgeted Balance Sheet at 31st March 19×2

	Cost £	Depn. £	Net £
Fixed Assets:			
Freehold property	30,000	—	30,000
Equipment	18,500	600	17,900
	48,500	600	47,900
Current Assets:			
Stock	12,200		
Debtors	12,000		
Bank balance	—	24,200	
Less Current Liabilities:			
Creditors	8,000		
Accruals—loan interest	100		
Overdraft	2,200	10,300	
WORKING CAPITAL			13,900
CAPITAL EMPLOYED			61,800
FINANCED BY:			
Capital			50,000
Add: Net profit			6,800
			56,800
Loan			5,000
			61,800

Note: The closing stock is calculated as follows:

	£	
Opening stock	9,200	
Purchases	27,000	
Total stock	36,200	
Less: Closing stock	12,200	
Cost of Sales	24,000	(40% of sales and work backwards)

Questions and problems

16–1   What is a budget?

16–2   List the advantages of budgeting.

16–3   What is the function of a budget committee?

16–4 Distinguish between 'operating' and 'capital' budgets.

16–5 What are limiting factors?

16–6 What is a 'master budget'?

16–7 Is the sales budget important? Why?

16–8 What is a cash budget?

16–9 On 1st January 1987 the Celtic Catering Supplies Co. was formed with a fully paid capital of £72,000 in £1 ordinary shares. The company has, in addition, taken out a temporary loan of £28,000 from the bank which it intends to repay with 10% interest per annum at the end of March 1987.
   In January the company purchased:

Premises	£40,000
Equipment	£16,000
Furniture and fittings	£12,000
Stock	£14,000

The estimated sales for the first six months were:

	£		£
January	4,500	April	30,000
February	18,000	May	32,000
March	23,000	June	34,000

Of these sales, ¾ were for cash and ¼ was paid for two months after sale.

Purchases for the period were estimated as follows:

	£		£
January	2,700	April	23,000
February	14,000	May	25,000
March	16,000	June	27,000

of which 20% were for cash and the remainder paid for one month later. Wages each month were estimated at £2,500 with no time lag.

Other expenses were estimated at £1,600 per month payable in the month concerned.

The company proposed to purchase additional furniture, £4,000, in March, and it expected to receive income from rented concessions at the end of June amounting to £2,700.

Construct a cash budget as it would have been drawn up for the six months January to June.

Comment on the results and state if you think the company made wise decisions.

What are the main objectives of cash budgeting?

16–10 The following information is presented in relation to the budgetary requirements of a small restaurant:

1. At 1st July 1983 the cash balance is forecast to be £7,000.
2. Forecast sales:

		£
May	1983	6,000
June	"	8,000
July	"	12,000
August	"	16,000

These figures are net of VAT, and there are no service or cover charges. Twenty-five per cent of each month's sales are anticipated to be on credit, of which 60% pay after one month and the remainder after two months.
3. The restaurant will work to a 60% gross profit and will replace stock during the month after it is used. Ten per cent of purchases will be cash, the rest on credit. One month's credit is to be taken.
4. Stock on 1st June 1983 was £5,000.
5. Expenses will amount to £36,000 per annum, which will be paid each month, except that this figure includes rent of £6,000 per annum which will be paid in advance once a year on 1st October.
6. Depreciation for the year of £2,400 will be charged.
7. In July an asset is to be sold for £200, book value £250, and is to be replaced by one costing £1,200.
8. A new extension costing £40,000 is nearing completion. Seventy-five per cent of this cost is payable in mid-July and the rest one month later.
9. A five-year loan of £20,000 is to be raised on 1st July to help finance this extension. Interest of 12% per annum is due twice a year and is to be paid in arrears. None of the capital is to be repaid until the end of the five-year term.

You are required to:
(a) Calculate whether the £20,000 loan will be sufficient to cover the cash requirement for July and August.
(b) Calculate the components of working capital, and comment on the net working capital position produced as at 31st August on the basis of the above information.

(HCIMA)

61–11 (a) Prepare the budgeted profit and loss account and budgeted balance sheet for the Dartside Restaurant for the three months ending 30th September 1986 from the following information:

Balance Sheet as at 30th June 1986

	£
Fixed assets at cost	10,000
Stock	1,000
Current account	2,000
Trade creditors	(1,000)
	12,000
Capital	10,000
Loan	2,000
	12,000

Cash Budget for 3 months ending 30th September 1986

		£	£
Sources	– Balance B/F	2,000	
	Cash sales	20,000	22,000
Applications	– Drawings	2,000	
	New equipment to be bought		
	on 30th September 1986	2,000	
	Trade creditors	10,000	
	Labour costs	5,000	
	Cash overheads	4,000	23,000
Balance C/F			(1,000)

(a) Depreciation will be 10% per annum on costs. Cost of sales will be 40% of sales. The trade creditors will be £2,000 (estimate) on 30th September 1986. The loan is at an annual rate of interest of 10% and the interest for the year is payable at the end of January.

(b) 'Good budgetary control is essential for the survival of a catering business.' Discuss this statement.

(HCIMA)

Index

Managerial Accounting in the
Hotel and Catering Industry

Contents